How to Get Planning Permission

An Insider's Secrets

by
Martin Gaine

Contents

Preface

Britain has the most intrusive householder planning system in the world. It exercises control over even the smallest developments – repainting your front door, putting up a satellite dish, or paving your front garden.

Because planning powers are spread over 365 councils in England and planning departments are harassed and poorly funded, whether your application is approved swiftly and efficiently, or languishes for weeks before being refused can be a matter of luck and location.

Permitted development (PD) adds extra complication. It grants a blanket planning permission, in advance, to every householder in the country for small and uncontroversial developments. Except that it doesn't. Flats don't have PD rights, nor do most houses in conservation areas, or most houses built after the Second World War. They are also subject to a long list of complicated tests and conditions. To most householders, permitted development complicates rather than simplifies the process of extending or enhancing their home.

Every year, thousands of upstanding, law-abiding citizens become subject to enforcement proceedings – accused of breaching planning control and facing the prospect of tearing down an extension or reversing some other form of development that they thought was PD or had planning permission. How to navigate these choppy waters?

Take professional advice. Just 0.01 percent (not an actual statistic) of homeowners and small developers employ the services of chartered town planners. Most take advice from the man down the pub or listen to the voice inside their heads. Too many hire the wrong designer and submit the wrong application. In most of the cases I deal with, the crucial mistake was made at the very beginning of the process, when the homeowner scrimped on the services of a decent designer and went into battle unprepared.

I am a gamekeeper turned poacher. I worked as a town planner at the Environment Agency and in local council planning departments, in a property development firm and as a private planning consultant, before finally setting up Just Planning (just-planning.co.uk), which specialises in helping householders and small developers who have run into planning problems.

As a council planner, I decided the fate of thousands of extensions and other small-scale developments, cheerily stamping a big, red NO almost as often as a begrudging, green YES. I can tell you that planners do get a little thrill from their power to end homeowners' dreams – it is sometimes the only perk of a job which gets a little samey, to put it mildly.

Designers and applicants get frustrated when councils refuse planning permission without really working with them to improve the application first. It is a fair point, but the reality is that planners do not have the time or the resources (or inclination) to do the designer's work for them. Planning policies are public information – it is important to look them up before you apply.

Council planners must shoulder some of the blame though. Some refusals are clearly, obviously, unfair. Other applications are refused because the planner has misunderstood the nature of the proposal or rushed the processing of the application. Some decisions are mean-spirited. Some planners think they are at war with applicants, protecting the integrity of the home front from dastardly extension incursions.

When I worked as a council planner, I saw countless people submit a half-cooked application and justifiably get refused, or submit a decent scheme and get refused unfairly, and then simply give up. Such refusals mean that people all around the country, having spent hundreds and thousands of pounds on their application, must go without the extension that would give their kids their own rooms or the family a large, bright breakfast room. Worse, they get permission for a compromise proposal that isn't really what they wanted.

It saddened me when I had to refuse applications for proposals that were badly designed or just not presented in a way that I could persuade my line managers to support, and then never heard from the applicant again. Did they give up entirely? In most cases, I could see the small changes that would have made their proposal acceptable. Planners are expected to give general advice on why an application is refused but can't give advice that should be coming from their architect or planning consultant. My planning decisions often delivered very poor outcomes and in many cases I wished I could have explained to applicants how to appeal my decision.

In late 2014, I applied for planning permission to extend my little ground floor flat in west London. I was working at the time as a planner for a different council, in the east of the city. It genuinely never occurred to me that I might be refused permission. I was an experienced planner; I understood the local policies and guidance, and the extension I was applying for was conventional and boring. I was so confident that I didn't bother to call the case officer and try to influence the decision.

My application was refused. The planner advised that I resubmit, significantly reducing the size of the extension. I did so, obtained permission, and carried out the works. Six months later, my next-door neighbour applied for an extension that matched exactly the one for which I had originally been refused consent (i.e. larger than what I had ultimately built). His application was approved by the same officer who had turned me down. To this day, I regret that I didn't fight harder to get the outcome I wanted. At the time, the experience opened my eyes to the impact that the random, unjustified decisions of individual planners can have on the humble householder and the rightful enjoyment of their homes.

I left council planning (and joined the dark side) because I wanted to help both the people who were submitting weak applications in the first place, with little hope of success, and the people who were being treated so unfairly by our failing planning system. In the former case, simple changes can make a bad scheme acceptable. In the latter, you must take the application away from the council altogether and have the decision reconsidered by a government inspector through a planning appeal.

My company, Just Planning, is an appeals specialist. I have personally submitted thousands of planning appeals and won most of them. I know how easy it can be to get permission for what you want, and how many people end up with something less than that. Our homes are our most valuable assets and the places where we spend a great deal of our time. An extension lasts forever (pretty much) and it is important to get it right.

This book is intended for householders who are engaging with the planning system and need some direction. It will also be of interest to designers and property developers, who also grapple with a complicated planning system. It starts with a rant on the failings of planning when it comes to smaller-scale developments. It goes on to set out six key steps on the planning journey: getting the right design, exploiting permitted development rights, understanding how planning decisions are made, applying tactically and effectively, appealing a refusal, and avoiding enforcement action. It ends with some hacks – the tips and tricks I have learned over the years that may smooth your passage through the planning maze.

Disclaimer: I provide general advice derived from my own experience over the years. It mostly applies to England and Wales – the planning systems are slightly different in Scotland and Northern Ireland (though the principles are the same). My advice is not intended to be exhaustive. Planning is a complex world, as you are about to find out, so always take professional advice that is bespoke to your situation, before relying on any of the information in the following pages.

You may notice that I refer interchangeably to "planners" and "case officers" – in both cases, I mean employees of the council who process and assess planning applications. For ease of comprehension (and through force of habit), I refer to the bodies that decide planning applications as "councils", though strictly speaking I mean "local planning authorities". I refer to the people who prepare and submit planning applications as "designers" – I avoid using the term "architect'" because not all the people who prepare and submit planning applications are fully-fledged architects (and they don't need to be) and the term "draughtsperson" seems awkward and clumsy. Terms that you might not be familiar with (planners love jargon!) are highlighted in **bold** and defined in the glossary at the back of the book.

Introduction:
What Is Wrong with UK Planning and Who Is to Blame?

Most homeowners have no real interest in the planning system, as such. It is complicated and bureaucratic and, unless you are a planning geek like me, very boring. However, if you want to alter or extend your home, you need to engage with it in some way. Even if you expect that the works you plan to carry out will not need planning permission, it is best to speak to the planners in order to establish that fact. Most homeowners will interact with the planning system at one point or another – this book arms you with the information you will need to make that interaction as painless as possible.

In this introduction, we explore how the planning system works and why it so poorly serves applicants, **case officers** (not always the villains), and the wider general public. The flaws in the British planning system present homeowners with challenges, but also with opportunities. Once you understand that planning is far from perfect, you will be much better placed to avoid the pitfalls and exploit the opportunities.

WHAT IS THE PLANNING SYSTEM?

Simply put, the planning system places restrictions on what you may do with your property where your actions may have harmful effects on the wider community.

It is obvious that some kind of control is necessary. Our little island is more cramped than many other places, we build our homes in high densities, and our long and glorious history has also left us a legacy of beautiful buildings. It is not just that our buildings are old, but our forebears grouped them in very pleasing arrangements – think of the symmetry of a row of identical Victorian terraced houses or a scattering of stone cottages in a Cotswolds village. It does make sense that we shouldn't be allowed to build what we like, where we like and it is true that this control should probably be more intrusive than in other countries, such as the United States, which have more space and, let's be honest, uglier buildings.

But the strange thing is that the British planning system isn't really very *British*. Our political and economic philosophy is essentially liberal and laissez-faire – we are a free-wheeling capitalist society wedded to the power of market forces. Excessive regulation is usually assumed to create distortions and inefficiencies. It is not clear how we ended up with a planning system that is so exceptionally rigid. Britons consider property rights to be sacrosanct, but at the same time your rights to do what your like with your own land and property are limited by planning controls. There is very little you can do to your home without needing express planning permission.

In most other countries, land is zoned and loose controls are put in place to limit the worst excesses of unrestricted development, but a lot of development does not need planning permission. Most small alterations do not need consent at all. The British planning system, however, is one of heavy state intervention in even the most minor alterations to a home.

The British media is endlessly critical of the planning system, but it tends to focus on large-scale schemes. Sometimes, the planners are unfairly maligned – the dithering over a third runway at Heathrow is the fault of indecisive politicians, not the planning system. I also think the planning system works reasonably well for large housing developments. The fact that it delivers monotonous estates of bland houses may be more a function of development economics and the limited imagination of large developers than the failings of council planners.

From my point of view, the main problem with the planning system is how poorly it serves the humble householder or small developer. The main reason for this is that these groups do not have the knowledge or the resources that larger developers marshal and deploy in order to get their applications through. Case officers (and the wider planning system) take advantage of this asymmetry in knowledge and power.

I have always been fascinated by small-scale planning – how householders extend their homes and how small sites are developed. Which is lucky, because that is all I was allowed to do when I worked in local government.

Pity the Planners

The tragedy of the UK planning system is that it locks up its planners in a tedious prison of single-storey rear extensions.

Spatial planning is about creating *places*. We planners are trained to understand how society and space interact and are told we will be creating and improving communities. We are taught to think big. Then we graduate, join a council planning department, and begin thinking very, very small.

According to the Ministry of Housing, Communities & Local Government, 90 percent of all planning applications are for minor applications (extensions and small commercial developments). The bulk of a council's planning team is made up of case officers who deal with householder applications: a daily, dispiriting diet of single-storey rear extensions and dormer windows. The UK planning system sucks the soul out of its planners.

I happen to enjoy the smallest applications – they are still a form of placemaking, and they allow you to help real people with proposals that are small in scale but really very important to them. I prefer a rapid turnaround of small applications to devoting months or years to a single, major scheme.

But it is not very glamorous, and it means that council planning departments do not attract the best and brightest new graduates. It is not a profession that rewards raw ambition. It is a job in public service, and although it does have its rewards, it is not as rewarding as it could be because it is focused too much on minor applications. The UK planning system therefore has a recruitment crisis – not enough young people consider it a worthwhile career option. This shortage of talent among our planners undermines the quality of service provided to applicants.

BLAME THE SYSTEM

In spite of this, most case officers work hard and are conscientious. Council officers in general care a great deal about their local patch and local authorities are a great place to work. Pretty much everything I know about how planning really works, I learnt from my colleagues in local councils. Ultimately the planners aren't at fault. The failure really lies with the system in which they have to operate.

It is overly prescriptive. In Britain, political control is centralised – Westminster and Whitehall have no real faith in local decision making. Councils are not well-resourced (especially in the post-austerity era) and rigid control is substituted for local discretion. Councils have the power to set out local planning policies and guidance, but demanding targets are set from above and the government keeps extending permitted development rights (allowing householder extensions without the need for planning permission) to take more and more proposals out of councils' hands.

And planning is, of course, highly political. Councillors are elected by, and answerable to, local residents. Local residents can, in turn, be vocal in their opposition to development in their area. Opposition to development is loud and focused and great pressure can be channelled from residents, through councillors to planning departments, even regarding relatively minor and small-scale applications.

In response to these pressures, planning departments develop a distinctive culture. As a planner, when you join a new council, your first job is to work out what that culture is. If the council hates **crown roofs** or two-storey side extensions, for example, and refuses to grant permission for them, you had better fall in line with this approach or find another job. Recommending approval of such applications against prevailing winds is possible in theory, but unsustainable in practice.

It is important to remember that case officers do not, strictly speaking, *decide* applications. They make recommendations that are either signed off by superior officers (under what are known as **delegated powers**) or considered by the planning committee of elected councillors. Case officers do not make a recommendation without an eye on who will make the final decision. It is not a good career move to recommend an application for approval if it will not be signed off by a line manager or if the recommendation is publicly overturned at committee. It is humiliating when a report is returned to you to be rewritten, making the opposite recommendation. (It also explains why so many applicants receive a refusal when the case officer had hinted that the application would be approved).

That isn't to say that case officers don't have discretion. A trusted case officer will have almost all of their recommendations signed off (especially if they cleave faithfully to the culture of their planning department). Some line managers barely check the plans or the officer's report before signing off on them. There is quite wide discretion for applications that have not generated any real local opposition.

COMPUTER SAYS NO...

The result of all this is that case officers are inclined to be reactive rather than proactive. There is no reward for daring to be original or creative and so it can be easier to refuse applications that to approve them. Neighbours and councillors often protest louder when an application is approved than applicants do when their application is refused.

Because case officers are cautious, conservative, and reactive (in order to avoid provoking resistance from senior officers, neighbours, and councillors), designers find it easier to submit cookie-cutter proposals than risk something more imaginative or adventurous. Innovation is not generally rewarded. The outcome is a "Carol Beer" stance on planning applications. Like the character in *Little Britain*, case officers say "computer says no" when applications do not comply directly and straightforwardly with the council's usual, habitual approach to other applications of the same type.

This creates a postcode lottery in planning. In the last quarter of 2020, the London Borough of Redbridge refused 47 percent of applications it received. Watford Council came second, refusing 40 percent. The councils of Tamworth, North East Lincolnshire, and Redditch, on the other hand, refused only one percent of applications[1]. The percentage of applications refused in England as a whole was 13 percent.

Applications that are acceptable in one area might be refused in a neighbouring council district. Proposals that were acceptable several years ago may no longer be, because a new cohort of councillors and senior planners has their own preferences and pet hates. Individual case officers make different decisions depending on their tenure, experience, and self-confidence.

Case officers respond to the pressures on them by avoiding interaction with applicants and neighbours. The reason I specialise in planning appeals (which are heard by a central government agency and not by local councils) is that I find communication with some local council planners to be intolerably painful. In my own local council, for example, case officers do not have direct

---

1   Source: Ministry of Housing, Communities & Local Government

telephone lines. One must instead ring the council switchboard and leave a message. Case officers have 48 hours to return the call. Often, they don't call back at all. Officers regularly ignore emails (something that would be considered entirely unacceptable in any other public-facing organisation) and occasionally respond in ways that are defensive, obstructive, or aggressive.

And yes, when I was a council officer, I too could be unhelpful. It was a response to the pressures of the job and the reality that incoming communications from applicants and neighbours generally brought with them fresh difficulties. People find planning applications extremely stressful (whether they are desperate for permission to be granted, or keen that it should not be) that they are not always very pleasant to deal with. However, the main reason I was unhelpful was because I *could* be – there is no strong culture of public service and no repercussions for providing a generally poor service.

BLAME THE HOUSING CRISIS?

Since we are in the blame game, the housing crisis deserves a mention. The general public and the government are broadly united in their view that the UK has a terrible shortage of new homes and that they must be built somewhere, as long as it isn't in the countryside or the **green belt**. The consequence of this is that we must squeeze ever more homes into existing towns and suburbs, often to the dismay of residents. It is an inevitable consequence of the state of current planning policy that areas with low densities and lots of open space will face considerable pressure from developers.

The housing crisis leads to high property prices, which encourage developers to undertake projects that would not normally be desirable or profitable, piling more pressure on residential areas. In a "normal" housing market, no sensible person would convert their garage into a studio flat, for example, because the value of the (sub-standard) new unit would be low. In London today, converted garages command high rents and resale values.

Government policy also feeds through to incentives when it comes to extensions. Eye-watering rates of Stamp Duty Land Tax (paid when you buy a home) create a perverse incentive to extend your home rather than move and buy a new home. In London and the southeast, in particular, you might pay £100,000[2] in stamp duty to move to a larger family home. That would pay for a lot of extensions. The result is that houses are often awkwardly extended and become oversized. The value of extra floorspace in £ per square foot is so high that the market doesn't punish homeowners (in terms of the market value of their home) for poorly conceived extensions. As a result, ugly developments proliferate.

SORRY, DEAR READER, BUT IT IS ALSO YOUR FAULT

As a planning consultant, I tend to think that the system is failing and that council case officers are too conservative and lack imagination. But when I was a council case officer, I found myself exasperated by the poor quality of submissions I had to deal with. Your opinion on where the blame lies for our failing planning system largely depends on your starting point.

Applicants and their **agents** must shoulder their fair share of the blame. Some really terrible planning applications are submitted to local authorities. Some are truly awful, with no hope of success. They waste the time and energy of the applicant themselves and of council officers. They exhaust neighbours who whip themselves up into a frenzy of objection. They are a huge waste of money.

Short-sighted homeowners hire the cheapest designers they can and, ultimately, get what they pay for. Designers charging low fees draw up bad quality plans without bothering to make sure that they are accurate, without any real attention to design or detail, and without checking in advance

---

2   According to www.home.co.uk, the average asking price for a four-bedroom house in London at the beginning of 2020 was £1,590,290. Stamp duty on the purchase of a property at this price would typically be £104,584.

whether they comply with local policies. This is a real drag on the system. It is bad enough that case officers spend so much of their careers assessing single-storey rear extensions, without most of the applications being substandard.

The following chapters will help you negotiate the planning system. They are laid out as a series of six steps. Steps 2–6 tell you how to make the most of permitted development rights, understand planning policies and processes, manage the application process, deal with a refusal, and be aware of the risks of planning enforcement. Following these steps is key to achieving a successful outcome.

However, if I could give applicants *just one* piece of advice, it would be to choose the best possible designer. I believe this is so important that I have made it Step 1 on our journey.

Step 1:
Hire the Right Designer

The biggest mistake people make when setting out to develop property is to choose the wrong **designer**. By designer, I mean the person who designs your extension, draws up your plans and submits and manages your planning application. Choosing the wrong one has two possible outcomes: either the council refuses planning permission and you have wasted time and money or, worse, you are granted permission for something that will be suboptimal. For a homeowner, this is an extension that disfigures your house, reduces its value, and doesn't meet your family's needs. For a developer, it is a development that doesn't make best use of the site and doesn't maximise profit.

Anyone can draw up plans and submit a planning application. There is no requirement to have basic design qualifications or competence. Most designers are not architects. But many of these "unqualified" designers are very good at their jobs – they specialise in smaller-scale proposals, design them well, are familiar with local planning policies, and have good relationships with the planners.

Others, however, are charlatans. They produce woefully poor plans that have little prospect of getting planning permission. In this chapter, I will help you distinguish between the good designers and the charlatans. Though the point of hiring a good designer is that they do the designing for you, at the end of the chapter I also explain what is meant by good design and explore some of the common mistakes people make when planning to extend their home.

How Do I Find the Perfect Designer?

The best designers for smaller-scale developments are local. They are likely to have a good understanding of the area, local council policy, and the proclivities of council planners.

Every council receives a disproportionate number of applications from well-established, local architects and designers; they have something of a relationship with the planners. This doesn't mean that the planners do them any favours, but it does mean that those designers may be able to get the case officer on the phone to be able to talk through any problems.

All councils keep a public record of planning applications on their website. To find the designers who are active in your area, navigate to your local council's website, click on "planning applications", and use the search function to bring up a list of all applications decided in the last 30 days. Take some time to work through a selection of applications that appear to be similar to yours. You may notice that a small number of designers appear again and again – these are the firms to add to your shortlist.

How Do I Spot the Charlatans?

Now you have a shortlist of designers, it's time to flush out the charlatans. There are four clues to help you separate the wheat from the chaff.

First Clue – Price

The first clue is price. You get what you pay for (most of the time, at least). Low prices are a red flag. A sum of £300 or £500 is not enough to compensate a good designer for visiting a property, providing advice, measuring the building, drawing up a full set of plans, revising them as needed, and submitting and managing the planning application. Spending small amounts on a designer is a false economy – the development will be poorly-conceived, there will be errors on the plans (that may make any planning permission you do obtain invalid), you will have no credibility with the planners, and you are much less likely to be granted permission. If permission *is* granted, the development may be difficult to build. You should expect to pay between £1,000 and £2,000 for a designer to prepare full, detailed planning drawings for an extension, and to submit and manage your application.

Although a low price is a good indicator of poor quality, a high price is not always a sign of excellence. I worked for a council where a majority of the applications for extensions were submitted by two architects, working for different firms, who monopolised the local market. One charged twice as much as the other (£2,000 to £3,000 for a relatively straightforward application). When applications were received from the cheaper architect, my colleagues and I barely glanced at them before recommending approval – he generally submitted thoughtful and sensible proposals that complied with local planning policies and guidance. He had great credibility and we felt bad on the rare occasion that amendments were required or an application of his was refused. When applications were received from the other, more expensive architect, my colleagues and I groaned, reached for our red pens, and began drafting our objections. His plans were poor quality and error strewn and he proposed developments that did not comply with local policies. In this example, the cheaper architect represented much better value. So, one must avoid low priced offerings, but higher prices do not necessarily signal virtue. How else can one identify the best designers?

SECOND CLUE – QUALITY OF DESIGN SUGGESTIONS

The second clue is the quality of their suggestions in respect of the design of the building and their knowledge of what will and will not be granted planning permission. The charlatans will simply ask you what you want and prepare plans accordingly. If you ask them whether you might be able to get permission for a 10-metre-deep extension rising three storeys high, they will nod sagely, suck on a pencil, and say they can't guarantee anything, but it is worth a try. If you ask them how it will be designed, they may look at you blankly and explain that it will have four walls, be built in brick, and have a tiled roof. If you ask about the internal layout or "flow" they may suggest you attach it to the end of your kitchen and access it through a door. If you express concerns about possible impact on a neighbour's window, they will say that the neighbour is too far away to be affected. If you ask them whether the proposal complies with local planning policies, they will smile reassuringly and say that they get permission for these kinds of extensions all the time.

A good designer will do just that – design. They will ask you what you are trying to achieve, what you need the additional living space for and how you would like the house to be configured. They will have a good understanding of how your house can be altered in a way that is sensitive to its original shape and proportions, and how to make best use of space. They will almost always push back and bring some of your dreams crashing down. Most homeowners, in my experience, want more than can realistically be achieved. Only confident designers will burst their bubbles. The best will find creative ways to meet your needs or will make suggestions that hadn't occurred to you before.

Designers need an iron will. Few homeowners ask for a simple extension that will sail through the planning process. Almost everyone wants to push the envelope. Many want an extension bigger than the largest extension on the street. Some want a combination of all the different extensions visible on other houses in their area, combined into one mega development. From the designer's point of view, the initial meeting with a prospective client is a beauty parade; crushing the homeowner's dreams is unlikely to result in a commission. So, beware the designer who agrees with all your suggestions and does not temper your aspirations.

Remember that the designer does not guarantee you will receive planning permission. Their commitment to you is to draw plans and submit the application. They can take no responsibility for the application being refused because planning processes are inherently uncertain. This can reduce their incentive to do a good job. They can draw up a bad scheme, knowing it will never get permission, and just tell you, when it fails, that it is the fault of capricious planners and a hostile planning system. Be very suspicious of the designer who agrees to submit whatever you ask them to. To work out whether lots of your prospective designer's applications have been refused, search on your local council's planning application website and try and find some of their recent applications.

Third Clue – Quality of Drawings

The third clue is the quality of their drawings. Don't ask them to send you examples, go on to a council planning website and find one of their recent applications. I appreciate that people who have never applied for planning permission before may not be familiar with scaled drawings, but most people have an instinctive sense of quality. A designer's plans are a kind of sales pitch – they are intended to persuade a planning case officer to grant permission. It is important that they are detailed and, well, pretty.

The worst plans are line drawings, like the stick men children draw, with no variation in line thickness and no shading. An example, from a case I dealt with, is shown in figure 1. It is clear, even to a layman, that these drawings lack detail and sophistication. The application was for a two-storey side extension and these drawings show the proposed front and rear **elevations**.

The extension doesn't appear to have been carefully designed and the drawing does not present the extension in its best light. The drawings aren't labelled (the front elevation is on top and the rear elevation below), and there is no scale bar. Poor quality drawings like this make it much less likely that permission will be granted and, even if it is, give you little to work from when it comes to building the extension. If permission was granted in this case, the homeowner would have been required to build the extension strictly in accordance with the plans, which may have been difficult when so little detail was incorporated. Failing to build in strict accordance with the plans leaves you open to **enforcement** action (see Step 6 for more on enforcement). I help hundreds of homeowners each year who inadvertently find themselves in this kind of stressful situation.

Your plans should accurately and comprehensively represent the building that has been drawn. There should be no errors. Floorplans and elevations should correspond. Differences in ground levels should be shown – if your garden is sloped, it should not appear flat on the drawing. You can't build a flat extension on sloping land – any planning permission granted on this basis would be invalid. All plans should have proper labelling and a scale bar.

Planning drawings and construction drawings are different. Planning drawings should not show foundations or the depth of insulation. Designers who show this information either don't understand the nature of planning drawings or are trying to make their work look more impressive to you.

Fourth Clue – Knowledge of Planning

The fourth clue is that a designer should be able to explain how they will manage the planning process and be able to clearly state what's included in their fee. Most designers love the pure, creative process of drawing plans (that's what they were trained for) but hate the grubby business of selling it to the planners. When quizzed, a good designer will tell you how they manage the planning application process and how they communicate with the case officer. Does the fee quoted cover include the designer's presence at the site visit (when the case officer comes to inspect the property), for example?

It is essential that your designer is aware of local planning policies and guidance or, at the very least, is aware that taking account of local policies is critical to success, and that they will have to research them as part of the design process.

You should have a clear understanding with your designer about what happens if the case officer wants the plans to be amended or if the application is refused. Are additional charges levied for revisions? Will the designer meet with the case officer after a refusal to get a good understanding of what might be acceptable? Are charges levied for a second, revised application? It is crucial that the designer does not feel that they can simply walk away at the end of the process if planning permission is refused. They must be willing to continue to work with you until permission is obtained.

Figure 1: Poor quality plans make it harder to get planning permission

Do I Need an Architect (Rather Than Just a Draughtsperson/Designer)?

Though we tend to describe anyone who prepares plans and submits applications as an **architect**, most people preparing plans for smaller applications are draughtspeople or designers, rather than fully-fledged architects. The Architects Act 1997 states that the title "architect" is protected and it can only be used in business or practice by someone who has had the education, training, and experience needed to become an architect, and who is registered with the Architects Registration Board (ARB).

Although architects are generally the best trained in the business, they are generally more expensive than their less-qualified colleagues, and some can be just as guilty as unqualified charlatans of preparing ill-conceived applications.

Plans prepared by architects are always of a high quality. They will be accurate and look impressive; they will usually have interesting design flourishes and make good use of space. This is because architects are design-led; their weakness can be a poor understanding of planning policies and guidance, as well as of what will and will not be granted permission. Case officers are used to receiving impressive sets of plans from talented architects who have not read local policies. If I were submitting an application for a relatively straightforward extension, I would prefer a competent local designer over a talented architect with no direct experience in smaller-scale planning applications in my local area.

Should I Hire a Planning Consultant (Like You)?

Actually, though it pains me to say it, there is usually no need to pay for the services of a **chartered town planner** (like me). However, if you choose not to employ a planner, ensure that your designer has a good understanding of local planning policies and a sense of whether or not your proposal will be successful. Too many designers prepare applications to their client's demands without considering whether the proposal will be granted permission. This leads to unnecessary refusals, and wasted time and effort.

Planning consultants are useful where the designer does not have specific knowledge of the way a particular council approaches planning applications. They are also useful if the proposal is especially complicated or controversial. Some designers hire me as part of the overall package they sell to the homeowner – a two-in-one service. In those circumstances, I advise on local policy and guidance, provide comments on the proposed plans, prepare a planning statement to justify the proposal, and ease the application through the planning system. Some design firms have qualified planners in-house.

Planning consultants are especially useful for applications that do not comply with local policy or guidance and where the application therefore needs to persuade the council to make an exception. We often work for clients who approach us after their designer has said something like, "you can't have a four-metre-deep extension, the council doesn't approve anything more than three metres." Planning consultants help in cases like these by checking the local policies, confirming whether or not the council has been granting permission for larger extensions, and advising whether an exception to usual practice or policy might be justified. There is more on this in Step 3 on **planning policies** and getting applications approved.

Planning consultants are also helpful for some of the trickier areas of planning. As we will see in the next chapter, permitted development is a minefield. New permitted development rights allowing homeowners to add two extra floors to their houses (from September 2020) are difficult to understand and exploit without the expert advice of a planning consultant, for example.

CASE STUDY: THE 'HOPELESS' FLAT CONVERSION

In 2019, Mrs Mansour decided that she wanted to convert her three-bedroom terraced house in north London into two separate flats. It was her retirement plan – she would live on the ground floor and earn some income by renting out the new first floor flat.

She hired a local designer, who measured up the house, prepared plans and submitted a planning application. On top of the cost of paying the designer for his time, she paid an application fee to the council of just under £500. Eight weeks later, the council informed her that the application had been refused.

Mrs Mansour contacted me for advice. I discovered that her house was in an area that the council had identified as suffering from "conversion stress" meaning that a large number of houses had been converted into flats, changing the "character" of the area, so the council would not grant permission for any more conversions. It had a clear planning policy to that effect in its local plan (its published collection of planning polices). A review of recent decisions revealed that the council had refused all applications for flat conversions in that area since the policy came into effect and, in the small number of cases where applicants had appealed the decision, they had not been successful.

Mrs Mansour's application therefore stood no chance of success and had been a waste of time. This was not necessarily the fault of the designer – he had never said that he would research local policies and similar local decisions before preparing the plans and submitting the application. However, by hiring a designer who was more familiar with local planning policies or seeking advice from a planning consultant before embarking on her project, Mrs Mansour would have saved time and money.

FORM V FUNCTION

Finding the right designer is the first step, but it is not quite enough. It is important for you, the homeowner, to have a good idea of what you want and to participate effectively in the design process. Pushing your designer to submit an application for something that just won't get consent is clearly counterproductive. You should spend some time rationalising your own thoughts about how you live in your house, what kind of extra space you need, and how it may be added without harming the appearance of the building or affecting your neighbours.

If the first big mistake homeowners make is choosing the wrong designer, the second is trying to get permission for the biggest possible extension, no matter how ugly. It is a strange impulse – why disfigure your house?

There is a classic tension in architecture between *form* (the size, shape and appearance of a building) and *function* (what it will be used for). If function is prioritised, the internal space is designed to meet the needs of the user, but the consequence can be that the outside appearance suffers. Conversely, if one focuses on creating a beautiful building on the outside, the space created internally may not work.

Most homeowners start with function. They want a certain amount, often quite a lot, of extra space. What it will look like from the outside is a secondary concern. Size matters, obviously, but big isn't always better when it comes to householder extensions. This is, of course, where the local council planners come in. They don't care what you are planning for the inside of your house, they are concerned about what it will look like from the outside.

At some point in the past, your house was carefully designed. Some thought was given to its size and scale, its proportions, and the choice of materials. It is likely that the elevations of your house are symmetrical and that it matches the others on the street, creating a harmonious "streetscene". Extending your home to incorporate a large volume of extra space clearly has the potential to create harm.

Monstrous Carbuncles

In 1984, Prince Charles was horrified by a proposed extension to the National Gallery, famously describing it as, "a monstrous carbuncle on the face of a much-loved and elegant friend." The proposal was duly scrapped. He didn't win the wider war, though. Despite the best efforts of our planners, thousands of carbuncles appear on the faces of properties up and down the country every year. Some extensions are truly horrible, and one wonders why someone would allow their home to be spoiled in that way (and how they were able to obtain planning permission!).

To a planner, the biggest carbuncles are those that can be seen from the street. Ugly rear extensions are much less of a problem – only a small number of misfortunate neighbours can see them. In the image in figure 2, the homeowner has achieved a very substantial increase in the size of their home by building a two-storey side extension. However, there are issues with its design. The **ridge** (the highest point) of the new roof reaches up to the top of the original chimney. The extension is too wide and should probably be stepped back a little from the front wall of the main house (so that it is subordinate, in the jargon). The new window does not match the windows in the original house and neither the bricks nor the tiles match those on the existing building. In this case it is likely that the homeowner obtained planning permission for a side extension but did not build it quite in accordance with the approved plans.

Figure 2: This side extension adds a lot of space but is poorly designed

In the example in figure 3, a series of awkward extensions have merged two neighbouring houses, of different architectural styles, together. The house on the left has an A-shaped gable roof. The roof has been extended on either side with the addition of two dormer windows (a dormer is a roof extension; side dormers would usually be permitted development and not require planning permission), one bigger than the other. It has what might be a third dormer, further back, that extends all the way to the side wall and roof of the neighbouring house on the right. It also has a large ground and first floor side extension (the ground floor painted white and the first floor red). Only its porch extension is proportionate and well-designed.

Figure 3: The various extensions to these two houses harm the streetscene

The house on the right has also been extended – its roof was originally hipped (i.e. it had a side slope), but it was built out and a loft conversion was created. These extensions are very poorly designed (or have not really been designed at all) and though they provide acres of extra space internally, they harm the appearance of the two houses and the wider streetscene. It is hard to believe that planning permission was ever granted for these extensions – it is likely that works were carried out without permission and may be subject to enforcement action.

Size Matters

Most disputes with council planners are about size rather than siting or design. In many cases where I advise clients to amend a proposal and resubmit, I tell them to make it smaller – often substantially smaller. In most of those cases, the error that the applicant has made is to try and maximise the amount of additional space they can have, rather than truly *design* their extension and find a balance between form and function. Acres of unused floor space in your new breakfast room will add nothing to your family's breakfasting experience. A smaller, more intimate space might be more enjoyable, brighter, and take less time to clean.

Living spaces have an appropriate size, determined by their function. Room sizes should be optimised, not maximised. Oversized rooms are not cosy or comfortable. There is no point in your bedroom being twice as large as it needs to be. The skills of a talented architect or designer are key here. They can create more with less and configure your house so that each room is the optimal size and the spaces are connected in a logical way, creating a natural flow through the building. Remember that building work is priced per square metre. A rear extension that is one metre deeper than necessary will cost you thousands of pounds more in building costs.

CASE STUDY: THE 'OPTIMAL' TWO-METRE EXTENSION

In 2017, Mr & Mrs Paterson purchased a tired, run-down property in Leeds. It was a standard 1930s three-bedroom, semi-detached house. The couple had three children and the house was not going to be big enough for them without extensions to provide an enlarged reception space downstairs and at least one extra bedroom and bathroom upstairs.

They had a budget of £80,000, which may seem generous, but does not go very far when it comes to house renovations these days. For this, they wanted to extend to the rear at ground floor level to a depth of six metres and convert the loft with a large rear dormer window (a dormer is a square roof extension). Both of these extensions would usually be permitted development (i.e. would not need planning permission).

They came to me for advice and I referred to them to a talented local architect with whom I had worked in the past. She recommended that they limit their ground floor rear extension to a depth of two metres and convert their existing loft without adding a new dormer window. She proposed a creative internal layout that made efficient use of the space, providing a large, open-plan kitchen/diner, and a new master bedroom suite in the converted loft space. This dramatically cut the cost of the build – householder extensions are priced per square metre and smaller extensions are therefore proportionately cheaper. The Patersons were initially sceptical of the idea of a 'miserly' two-metre rear extension but were delighted with the final result.

LOOK AT YOUR HOUSE AFRESH

If you are thinking of extending or reconfiguring your home, you should start by taking a long, hard look at your house from the outside. You may not have looked at it properly since you bought it and moved in. You rush to and from it every day, spend much of your time inside it looking out, and just don't *see* it anymore. It's an invisible constant – part of your everyday.

Examine it from all angles. Cross the road and look at it from a distance. Work out what the original designer was trying to achieve – does it have original features, a certain symmetry, a particular choice and mix of materials? Examine how any existing extensions relate to the house – do they work? Do they fit in with the original architecture? Does the internal space they provide connect well with the original house? Think about how you use the house. Identify which spaces are most commonly used and which rooms or areas are almost abandoned.

Then look at your neighbours' houses. In most English streets, the houses are similar to each other. If the streetscene is attractive and harmonious, what creates that harmony? Is it a repetition of building sizes and styles? Which neighbours have successfully extended and what makes their extensions successful?

Before approaching designers, it is good to have a clear sense of how your property was originally designed and built, what works and what doesn't in terms of the quality of accommodation it provides, and what the wider streetscene is like. Ultimately, you want an attractive house. You need a good designer so that the extension complements the building and fits in well with the streetscene. An eyesore built onto the back or the side of your house will reduce its value and do nothing to improve your living conditions. Applying for something bigger and uglier than it needs to be sets up an almost inevitable battle with the planners, who see themselves as holding back the tide of poor design.

Battles with the planners are my bread and butter, but you can avoid them altogether by hiring the right designer and keeping your extension as small (and sensitively designed) as possible.

STEP 1 SUMMARY

1. Finding the right designer is the key first step to extending your house. Local designers are often best – use your council's planning search function to see which designers are actively submitting applications in your area.
2. Be wary of designers who are either very cheap or very expensive. Do not choose the cheapest or most obliging designer – it is a false economy to scrimp on this stage of the process.
3. Expect your designer to have thoughtful suggestions about how your house may be extended.
4. Assess the detail and attractiveness of a sample set of the designer's drawings.
5. Quiz the designer on what local planning policies and guidance will apply to your proposal and how they will manage the planning application process.
6. Curb your ambitions – size doesn't always matter and there should be balance between the internal space created and the appearance of the extended house from the outside.

KEY QUESTIONS TO ASK A PROSPECTIVE DESIGNER

1. What is their experience of similar applications in your area?
2. Can they provide details of similar, successful, applications that they have worked on (you can look up details of these applications on the council's planning website)?
3. What local planning policies and guidance will the case officer apply when assessing the application?
4. Does their fee include attendance at the site visit and any revisions to the plans that might be requested by the case officer?
5. What support will they provide if the application is refused?

Step 2:
Exploit Permitted Development Rights

You have thought long and hard about how you want and need to change your home. You have searched high and low for the best designer for the project (having flushed out the charlatans). Now, it is essential to get to grips with **permitted development** (PD). Firstly, because planning permission may not be required at all for what you have in mind and secondly because permitted development is a very complex and ever-changing area, which many homeowners (and planners and builders) misunderstand, leading to expense, hassle, and heartache.

What Are Permitted Development Rights?

Permitted development rights allow you to carry out certain types of development without the need to apply for planning permission. In England, they are set out in the General Permitted Development Order (the GPDO), legislation that grants planning permission in advance for various developments, subject to limitations.

Most of you will have heard of PD rights for domestic extensions – almost all householders in the country can extend to the front, side, rear, and on the roof without applying for permission. In recent years, there has also been a big increase in the PD rights available to property developers to change shops, offices, and other premises into residential units (mostly because the government doesn't trust the mainstream planning system to deliver enough new homes fast enough). In late 2020, new rights were added to the GPDO to enable whole extra floors to be added to existing buildings.

We must embrace any opportunity that allows us to avoid having to ask bureaucrats for permission to develop our own property. Broadly speaking, PD rights are much more generous than what might be achieved through mainstream planning. For example, you may get a much bigger extension (if size is what you are after) under PD than under a full planning application.

PD rights can therefore be a silver bullet and once you and your (carefully selected) designer have decided what kind of development you want, the first step is to establish whether you can achieve some or all of it by making use of PD rights, therefore circumventing the power of council planners to say no.

But beware! PD is a minefield. Some houses don't have PD rights at all (because they are listed buildings or in a conservation area, or because those rights were removed, for example). Flats have almost no PD rights. And the limitations and conditions set out in the PD legislation can be difficult to interpret. Never, ever assume that what you are proposing is PD and that you may press ahead without a care – you are strongly advised to prepare plans and seek confirmation from the council that your plans meet the requirements of the GPDO (and you will therefore still need the good designer you found in

Step 1). More on PD pitfalls later. First, let's look at the history of PD rights and what they can do for you.

Why Were Permitted Development Rights Introduced?

I said in the introduction that the planning system, with its lofty aims of creating better places, is actually groaning under the weight of thousands of applications for single-storey rear extensions to houses. PD was intended to free up the planning system by removing these uncontroversial, small-scale applications from the planning system altogether, thus liberating planners and homeowners, encouraging certain limited types of development, and setting a torch to red tape.

Is that how it worked out? Sadly, no. It is a rich irony of government action that legislation, systems, and controls that were introduced to reduce red tape simply seem to have created more fog and confusion. The introduction of PD has really just created a parallel planning system, meaning that applicants and their agents have to try and understand two competing ways of carrying out development as well as figuring out whether to use PD or apply for planning permission. Applying for planning permission is a simple concept. PD rights, subject to hard and fast rules set out in legislation, are much more difficult to understand.

Worse, policymakers can't resist the temptation to ratchet up the complexity. The government tinkers with the legislation every year. Disputes between applicants and councils about what is and is not PD reach the courts, and court decisions create legal precedents that change how the legislation should be applied. Much of my work involves keeping on top of the PD regulations so that I can properly advise clients. I am grateful to the government for keeping me in business, but PD has not liberalised the planning system in the way that it was intended to.

The recent creation of PD rights for the conversion of commercial premises into dwellings has been a boon for developers, especially smaller developers (volume housebuilders still chase large greenfield sites). These rights strip out the usual planning requirements – that the new units provide an element of affordable housing, for example – with the aim of delivering large numbers of new homes quickly. In that respect, they have been successful – huge numbers of new homes have been created, mainly through **office-to-residential conversions**, though many of these are of questionable quality. Like householder PD rights, though, they are a parallel planning system – the government is increasing housing supply by sidestepping the planning system, rather than reforming it.

What Is the GPDO?

PD rights are set out in the **General Permitted Development Order** (the GPDO), a statutory instrument that grants planning permission for specific types of development. The first GPDO came in to force in 1948, just after the birth of the modern planning system itself. It gave homeowners the right to erect outbuildings for keeping poultry and livestock (as long as the buildings were no taller than 10 feet and had a capacity of no more than 1,000 cubic feet) and to build fences up to seven feet tall. These rights reflected immediate post-war needs – encouraging food production in a time of rationing. There was, incidentally, a permitted development right allowing "cat's-meat" and tripe shops to change to "any type of shop". This may have been more of an encouragement than a right.

From there, the GPDO grew incrementally and became ever more complex. Householders now have a wide range of permissions for extensions, new windows, cladding and satellite dishes. There are 30 classes of development exempt from planning control (including, for example, works carried out by telecoms companies, railways, and public utilities) and a complicated set of conditions and limitations to each. There are also many circumstances in which some properties do not have permitted development rights at all.

There have been eight versions of the GPDO (1948, 1959, 1963, 1973, 1977, 1988, 1995, and 2015). Each version was amended on an almost annual basis. The GPDO 1995, which is the GPDO I worked with for most of my council planning career, was amended 21 times. The most recent version, the GPDO 2015, was amended in 2016, 2017, 2018, 2019, 2020 and 2021.

Seizing the Opportunities Presented by PD

Having spent the last few pages complaining about the complexity surrounding PD, it is time to consider the opportunities it presents. For homeowners, the real advantage of PD is not that it saves you the trouble of applying for planning permission – we will see in later chapters that householder planning applications are not too complicated and take around the same amount of time and effort – it is that permitted development rights are pretty generous, meaning that you can build extensions for which councils would not normally grant you planning permission.

This is a crazy contradiction. On the one hand, the government is determining, at a national level, that some forms of development are so minor and uncontroversial that they don't need full planning permission. On the other hand, councils that receive planning applications for these developments are refusing them. It is for this reason that, when extending, you should always explore your PD rights first.

What Are the Main PD Rights for Householders?

PD rights for England are set out in Schedule 2 of the GPDO. Householder extensions and alterations are covered by Part 1 of that Schedule. Different types of extensions are set out in categories: Class A relates to single-storey rear extensions; Class B to roof alterations and so on, as follows:

Class A	covers the enlargement, improvement or alteration of a house, such as rear or side extensions, as well as general alterations, such as new windows and doors.
Class AA	covers the extension of a house upwards to add one or two extra storeys.
Class B	covers additions or alterations to roofs that enlarge the house, such as loft conversions involving dormer windows.
Class C	covers other alterations to roofs, such as re-roofing or the installation of roof lights/windows.
Class D	covers the erection of a porch outside an external door.
Class E	covers development within the curtilage of the house (mostly sheds and outbuildings).
Class F	covers the provision of hard surfaces within the curtilage of the house, such as driveways.
Class G	covers the installation, alteration or replacement of a chimney, flue or soil and vent pipe.
Class H	covers the installation, alteration or replacement of microwave antennae such as satellite dishes.

As I have explained, the rights are not limitless – your extension is only PD if you meet the very specific criteria set out in the GPDO. Like all legislation, the GPDO is written in legalese and is therefore a little opaque, though if you read it slowly and carefully it is not as impenetrable as it first seems.

Helpfully, the government has published Technical Guidance to accompany the GPDO. This explains in simple language, and with use of diagrams, what is and is not permitted under the GPDO. The government also has a helpful online resource, called the "interactive house" which allows you to interact with a representation of a typical house to see how it might typically be extended. Interacting with the "house" is like playing a computer game and is about as fun as the householder planning system gets. Links to the GPDO, the Technical Guidance and the interactive house are provided in the Planning Resources section at the end of the book.

Remember that the GPDO legislation itself is the authority on PD rights – the Technical Guidance and interactive house are resources that seek to guide readers and are not an authority in themselves. Never proceed with a development without being sure that your development is PD (more on this later in the chapter).

The following sections summarise the main PD rights for householders. This is not exhaustive and only sets out the main limitations. Readers are strongly advised to obtain comprehensive and up-to-date advice (perhaps from the lovely planners at just-planning.co.uk) before leaping into a JCB and starting to dig foundations.

Class A: Side and Rear Extensions

Are there any houses left in England that do not have a single-storey rear extension built under PD rights?

By far the mostly widely-used PD right is the ability to extend to the rear at ground floor level. Older houses had narrow galley kitchens, or no kitchens at all, and all of us now want large, open-plan living spaces opening onto the garden.

There is a right under Class A (Part 1, Schedule 2) of the GPDO to extend to the rear to a depth of three metres on a terraced or semi-detached house and to four metres on a detached house. The extension must be from the original rear wall of the house and must not project (stick out) to the sides. It can be no more than three metres high to the **eaves** (where the guttering hangs) and no taller than four metres at its highest point (the apex of the roof). An example of the kind of single-storey rear extension allowed on a terraced or semi-detached house is shown in figure 4.

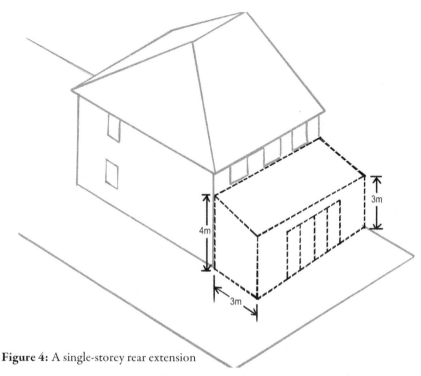

Figure 4: A single-storey rear extension

The extension cannot take up more than 50 percent of the **curtilage** of the site (that is, the site area excluding the footprint of the original house – generally the front and rear gardens). Materials must match the existing building (i.e. if your house is built in red brick, your extension should, in most cases, be built in a similar brick).

Class A also allows you to build to the rear over two storeys, but a requirement that the entire structure be set two metres away from the side boundaries rules it out for most homeowners.

Side extensions can be no wider than 50 percent of the width of the original house and must project to the side only. You cannot build to the side if your side wall faces a street (because you have a corner plot, for example). Note that it is not usually possible to erect a combined side and rear (known as a "wrap-around") extension because the total width of the combined extension would normally exceed 50 percent of the width of the house. An example side extension is shown in figure 5.

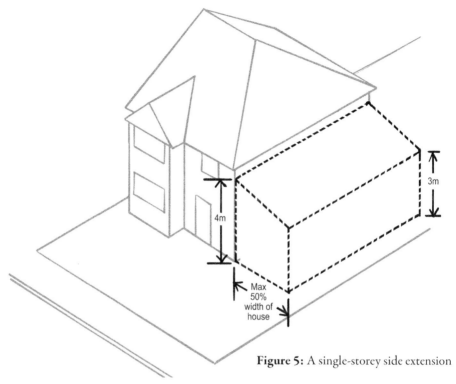

Figure 5: A single-storey side extension

PD rights are restricted on Article 2(3) land, which covers conservation areas, **Areas of Outstanding Natural Beauty (AONB)**, the Broads, National Parks, and World Heritage Sites. Under Class A, houses on Article 2(3) land cannot be extended to the side, cannot be extended to the rear at first floor level, and cannot be finished with external cladding.

Why Can't I Have a Ground Floor Extension if My Back Wall is Stepped?

The GPDO is full of quirks and oddities and it is these that trip up many homeowners (more on this later in the chapter). One of these is that houses that do not have a straight or flush rear wall (i.e. it is stepped or L-shaped), cannot have a full-width rear extension under PD. Case law has established that this kind of extension is not just a rear extension, but also a side extension (because the stepped rear elevation creates a length of side wall) and Class A limits the width of side extensions to no more than 50 percent of the main house.

If your rear elevation is stepped because of a later extension, that extension can be demolished. However, if the "step" is original to the house, your proposed extension as a whole can be no greater than 50 percent of the width of the main building.

It can still be worth applying for this kind of extension because some case officers do not fully understand this issue or overlook it when assessing an application. If refused, however, there would be no point in appealing the decision.

CLASS A ON STEROIDS: LARGER HOME EXTENSIONS

In 2013, the government beefed up Class A PD rights for single-storey rear extensions by doubling their permitted depth to six metres for terraced and semi-detached houses (as shown in figure 6) and eight metres on a detached house. It was partly a response to calls from homeowners to be able to build modern, cavernous, open-plan kitchen/family rooms, and partly an effort to give the flagging economy a boon in the slow years after the global financial crisis by setting homeowners to work on new building projects.

Initially, this was intended to be a permitted development right like any other (i.e. a simple adjustment to Class A to substitute the increased depth limits for the existing) but the government listened to concerns that some of these extensions might negatively affect neighbours through a loss of light and outlook, so it introduced a light-touch application process (known as the **neighbour consultation scheme**) by which applicants must first seek **prior approval** from their local council.

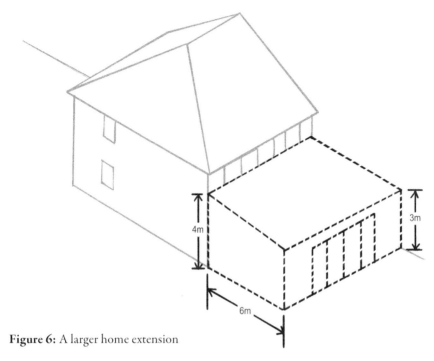

Figure 6: A larger home extension

The prior approval application process is much more straightforward than a planning application. The applicant must submit a short application form or covering letter, a block plan showing the location of the extension (no elevations or detailed drawings required) and (since 2019) a fee of £96. The council consults adjoining neighbours and then, if none of them object, must inform the applicant that prior approval is not required. In other words, if neighbours do not object, the council has no power to refuse the application and the extension to the depth proposed is permitted development.

If a neighbour does object, the council must assess the development in terms of its likely impact on all of the adjoining neighbours (not just the one who objected). The council cannot assess the extension on any other planning grounds (such as its design, impact on the streetscene, flood risk etc). If the council decides that the extension will harm a neighbour's amenity (typically in terms of overshadowing or a loss of outlook), it may refuse prior approval and your extension will not be considered permitted development.

Council planners (and I was working as one when the measure was introduced) were aghast at these new measures. For decades, almost every council in the country had determined that, as a rule of thumb, extensions of more than three metres deep, on a terraced or semi-detached house, were likely to harm neighbours. Most planners had spent some part of their career refusing applications for anything deeper than this. At the stroke of a legislative pen, the government had decided that this approach was wrong and that, in future, planners would have very limited power to assess or refuse permission for much larger structures.

Many authorities routinely refuse permission for any extension deeper than three or four metres where a neighbour has objected and they are therefore empowered to assess the application. At Just Planning my colleagues and I appeal dozens of these applications each year, with a high success rate.

In fairness to council planners (and bearing in mind that I used to be one), it is true that ground-floor rear extensions to a depth of six metres or eight metres seem oversized and, in pure design terms, disproportionate to most houses. An architect would never design a house with a six-metre-deep rectangular box sticking out of the back. But homeowners love them. The PD right grants permission for *up to* six or eight metres, but the vast majority of applications are for the full allowance. Six-metre-deep extensions to terraced houses are now a very common (and let's be honest, pretty ugly) feature of the rear gardens of most streets in built-up areas of England.

Remember the importance of good design and speak to your designer before following the herd. Do you really need a kitchen/reception room that is six metres long? Will it be light enough inside? Will the space relate well to the rest of the house, or will it unbalance your living space? Will the room be comfortable and cosy, with clearly defined spaces, or will you be eating your cornflakes in an aircraft hangar? Remember that deeper extensions are more expensive to build as building projects are priced per square metre.

It is worth noting that **larger home extensions** are not possible for houses on **Article 2(3) Land** (including conservation areas).

It is also very important to understand that you cannot start work on a larger home extension without first getting approval. Applications for prior approval are just that – your approval is not valid if you did not obtain it *prior* to starting work. If the case officer carries out a site visit and sees that you have already dug the foundations, your application will be refused. The same is not true of a conventional planning application – it is assessed in the same way whether you have started work or not. You may start work if you wish, but will be at risk of having to undo the work if later refused permission.

As a side note, this prior approval process for larger home extensions can trigger and exacerbate neighbour disputes. With a conventional planning application, a neighbour objection is not usually decisive – the proposal is assessed against planning policies and approved if it is acceptable, irrespective of the neighbours' opinions. For a larger home extension, the neighbours' views are key – the council cannot even assess the proposal if there are no objections. From my time as a council planner, I estimate that around 70 percent of proposals sail through without objection. However, relations between neighbours were harmed in cases where an objection scuppered a homeowner's plans to extend.

CLASS B: HIP-TO-GABLE ROOF EXTENSIONS AND REAR DORMER EXTENSIONS

The second most useful permitted development right is the ability to add an extra floor to a building through roof extensions. These are covered by Class B, Part 1, Schedule 2 of the GPDO.

A **hip-to-gable** roof extension involves the removal of the side slope to a roof and the creation of a gable end, in order to increase the volume of the roof, as shown in figure 7.

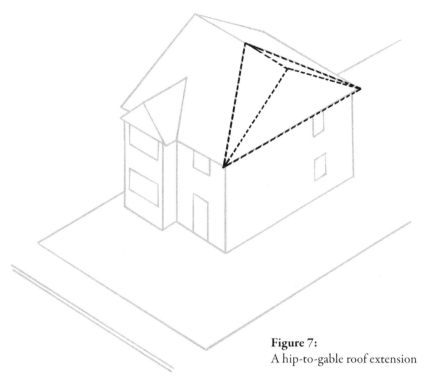

Figure 7:
A hip-to-gable roof extension

A rear **dormer** extension is the removal of part of the rear roof slope and the creation of a box-shaped rear extension to create additional living space, as shown in figure 8.

These developments can be carried out together under Class B (with front rooflights added under Class C) to create almost a full additional floor of living space. Typically, homeowners add one or two additional bedrooms with an en-suite shower room.

Such extensions may add no more than 40 cubic metres of volume to a terraced house and 50 cubic metres to a semi-detached or detached house. Dormers can only be at the rear or the side of the house, cannot rise higher than the ridge (the very top of your existing roof), and must be set back 20 centimetres from the eaves (the end of the roof slope, where your gutters hang). The materials you use must be "similar" to those on the existing property (this creates a problem for creative homeowners who would like timber or zinc cladding). Class B rights are not available on Article 2(3) Land (mainly conservation areas).

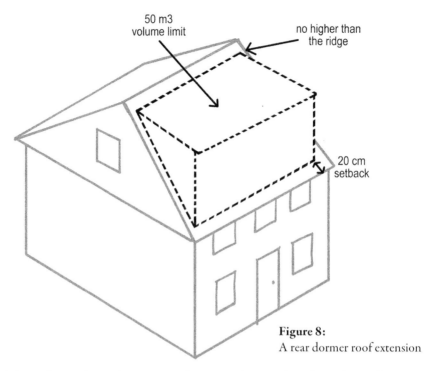

Figure 8:
A rear dormer roof extension

The cubic volume limit is tricky to understand and apply, and trips up applicants and their designers. If you are planning to build a roof extension, ensure your designer understands how to calculate the increase in the volume of the roof correctly. It is important to have very accurate and precise plans. If the roof has been measured incorrectly, and the dormer you build ultimately adds more than 40/50 cubic metres to its volume, you are at risk of enforcement action, with the possible consequence that you would have to demolish your extension. This may sound overly dramatic, but I deal with dozens of such cases each year.

Among planners, dormer loft conversions are the most controversial of the permitted development rights. By any objective measure, full-sized box dormers of the kind visible in figure 9 are disproportionate to most buildings, are ugly, and represent poor design. They make a mockery of the idea that permitted development rights only allow minor alterations. They are, however, massively popular with homeowners who need extra bedrooms for growing families and really don't care about what their house looks like when you crane your neck up and look at it from the garden. In the battle between form and function (discussed in Step 1), large box dormers represent the triumph of function over form.

Figure 9: Large "box" dormers are a common feature of residential areas

There has been a pandemic of dormer loft extensions in England and there are few people in the country who can look out of their rear window and not see at least one dormer extension on a neighbour's roof. It is partly because most houses built in the nineteenth and twentieth centuries were designed to have three bedrooms, one a box room, with the intention that children would share. Modern families want more space – larger rooms, extra bathrooms and no need to share bedrooms. It is expensive to move (thanks largely to punishing rates of stamp duty, a tax on growing families) and loft conversions are the quickest and easiest way to add a couple of extra bedrooms, turning a three-bedroom semi into a five-bedroom townhouse.

For higher value properties subject to disproportionately high rates of stamp duty, it is cheaper to extend than to move – a £70,000 loft conversion is much better value than a stamp duty tax bill of around the same amount.

This severely distorts the market – in some areas it is hard to find an un-extended three-bedroom semi – and homeowners should beware that the financial returns on roof level extensions are very low. Some people find that the tens of thousands they spend on their shiny new extensions is not returned in the increased value of their home.

"Double Dormers" under Class B

Many Victorian houses have **outriggers** – two storey rear projections connected to the back of the house. Class B allows dormer extensions that not only occupy the rear roof-slope of the main house but also project over the roof over any outrigger, as shown in figure 10. These dormers are known as "double" or "L-shaped" dormers and, though fairly large and ugly, they allow much more floorspace to be added at roof level.

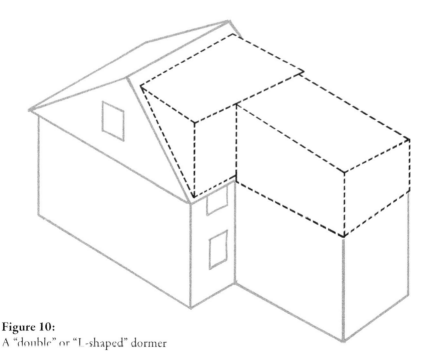

Figure 10:
A "double" or "L-shaped" dormer

CLASS C: ROOFLIGHTS

Class C allows rooflights (commonly known as Veluxes, after the well-known manufacturer) to be installed in the roof, as shown in figure 11. It requires that they do not stick out more than 150 millimetres from the surface of the roof and that, if they are on a side roof slope, they are obscure-glazed (i.e. have frosted glass) and cannot be opened. This is to protect neighbours from overlooking.

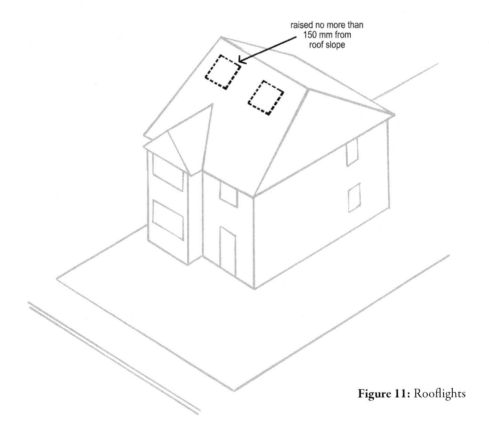

raised no more than
150 mm from
roof slope

Figure 11: Rooflights

Class D: Porches

Porches can be built outside any external door and can have a floor area of three square metres and a maximum height of three metres. Porches cannot be built within two metres of the boundary of the property with the highway (i.e. must be set two metres away from the road), as illustrated in figure 12.

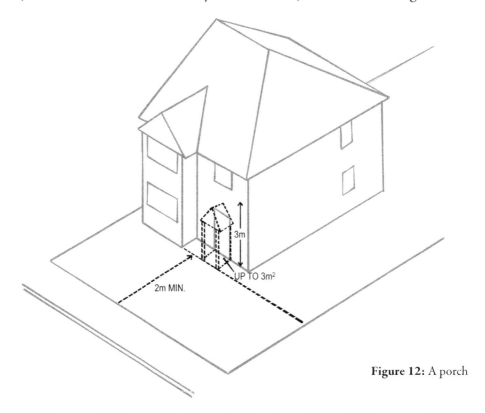

3m

UP TO 3m²

2m MIN.

Figure 12: A porch

Planners dislike porches, householders love them. Adding a porch gives you somewhere to store shoes, coats, brollies, and pushchairs, and somewhere to shelter from the rain while fumbling for your keys. However, a poorly designed porch can look like a pimple on the property and the larger the porch, the angrier the pimple. If you are on a street where all the houses are the same (a uniform pattern of development in planner-speak), a porch on one house can look out of place. If complying with the PD restrictions, you are free to build without the planners' interference, but it is still a good idea to give some thought to its size, roof design and the choice of materials, so that it enhances, rather than diminishes, the appearance of your home.

CLASS E: OUTBUILDINGS

Continuing the theme of controversial PD rights, outbuildings are a new frontier in the permitted development wars.

Householders naturally need outbuildings – a small, detached garage for their car or a simple wooden shed for garden tools. However, permitted development rights allow for a structure occupying 50 percent of the curtilage of the site excluding the original house (basically the grounds around your house), with some restrictions on height and siting – mainly that the outbuilding cannot be more than 2.5 metres high if it is located within two metres of any of the site boundaries, as shown in figure 13. The outbuilding cannot sit forward of your front wall – i.e. you cannot put a garage in your front garden, even though, for some properties, that is the most natural place for it.

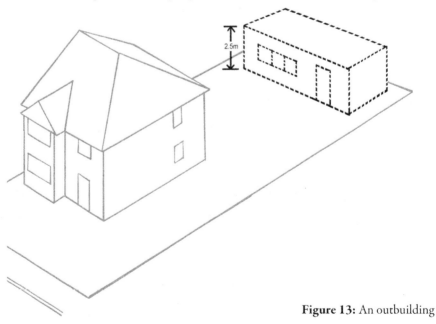

Figure 13: An outbuilding

The 50 percent limit is clearly rather generous – few homeowners really want a storage shed that takes up so much of the land around their house. But it allows some people to create valuable extra space – a gym, home office, swimming pool or a large garage to house a collection of classic cars.

Like six-metre-deep rear extensions and large dormers, council planners hate this permitted development right. In response, they have been known to say that larger outbuildings are not in fact permitted development. They argue that larger structures do not meet the requirement set out under Class E that the building be "reasonably required" (the council argues that the development is much larger than what a family might reasonably need), or try to suggest that the homeowner does not intend it to be "incidental" to (directly connected to their normal day-to-day use of) the main house.

It is therefore a little risky to build an outbuilding under your permitted development rights without seeking confirmation from the council that they do consider your proposal to be permitted development (see more below on applications for a Certificate of Lawfulness). If the council refuses to agree that your proposed outbuilding is permitted development, you should appeal – Just Planning has a near 100 percent success rate on these kinds of appeals.

Outbuildings have a poor reputation in the planning community. They have been tarnished by the small numbers of dodgy landlords who build a "gym" in the garden (complete with toilet and shower for use after a workout as well as a little kitchen for mixing up those protein shakes) and then rent out the building to tenants as a "studio flat". **Beds in sheds** are a hot political issue and a number of councils have received special funding from the government to tackle them.

Some faultless homeowners have been caught up in this campaign, especially those who have moved teenagers or elderly relatives into outbuildings, using them as an annexe. A family annexe is a use connected to the main house and it is not the creation of an entirely new dwelling for commercial purposes, so is it covered by Class E?

Can I Build an Annexe for Granny?

Class E allows the erection of outbuildings under permitted development, but not for use as primary living accommodation (i.e. as a bedroom, living room or kitchen). In short, no, you cannot build an outbuilding and move your granny in.

However, there is a loophole. As long as the original purpose of the outbuilding was not as primary living accommodation, its later use as such is PD. In other words, if an outbuilding was built and used as storage (or a gym or a home office) for some time, it could then subsequently be used as a bedroom or living room. To be clear, the living accommodation in the outbuilding would have to be connected to the use of the main house. In other words, you can move a stroppy teenager in there, as long as he uses the main house for meals and other parts of his day-to-day existence. Creating an entirely separate self-contained dwelling would require full planning permission.

CASE STUDY: LADY TARA'S GYM, OFFICE, SAUNA, AND CLASSIC CAR GARAGE

Lady Tara's handsome country house is located in the green belt, where new development is generally not allowed. However, houses in the green belt have the same permitted development rights that houses outside it have. This is another anomaly of our planning system – planning permission may not be granted for extensions or outbuildings in the green belt, but they can still be built using permitted development rights.

Lady Tara wanted to construct a new building in the sprawling grounds of her property. It was to contain a home office for her and her husband, a gym (with sauna and shower room), and storage for her collection of five classic cars. She submitted a Certificate of Lawfulness application to the council, requesting confirmation that the proposal was permitted development.

The council refused the application. They agreed that it met the specific criteria set out in legislation, apart from the stipulation that it be "reasonably required". The council argued that the size of the proposed building, which had an area of 170 square metres, exceeded what a family would reasonably need in a domestic outbuilding.

Lady Tara approached Just Planning for help. We appealed this decision on her behalf, pointing out that the submitted plans clearly showed how each part of the building would be used and demonstrating that each of these proposed uses was legitimate – a home office, gym, sauna, and car garaging are all domestic activities connected to the main house. We also pointed out that, although the outbuilding was large, it was not disproportionate to the house itself and its extensive grounds. The appeal was successful and Lady Tara is delighted with her new outbuilding.

The New Class AA: Upwards Extensions

As I mentioned earlier, some permitted development rights make the planning system more complicated, not less. The new Class AA, which came into force in September 2020, takes the biscuit. It allows homeowners to add up to two extra floors to an existing house, extending straight upwards, as indicated in figure 14. However, it is subject to so many limitations and conditions that few homeowners will benefit. I have had a flood of enquiries since the new rule came into effect, mostly from people who had previously been refused permission for an extension and hope that they can now try again. However, it is no silver bullet – I have advised most clients that they are unlikely to be in a position to take advantage of it.

Class AA allows two storeys to be added to a two-or-more storey house, or one storey to a bungalow. The extension must be directly above the existing house and only on the main body of the building (it is not possible to extend parts of the house that stick out to the front, side or rear, even if those projections are part of the original design of the house). One cannot extend a house that was initially created through some other permitted development right (an office-to-residential conversion, for example) or a house that was constructed before 1 July 1948 or after 28 October 2018. There are also limitations on the height of the extended building and the internal ceiling height of the additional storeys.

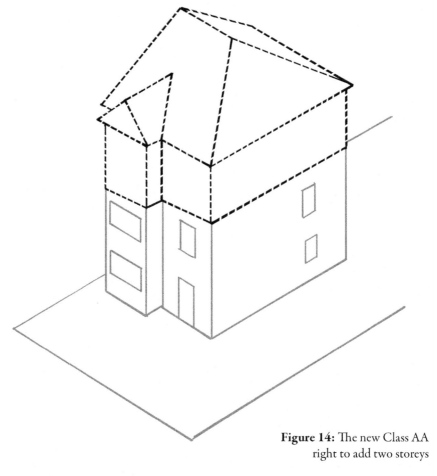

Figure 14: The new Class AA right to add two storeys

Like the larger home extensions discussed earlier (allowing you to extend to the rear at ground floor level to a depth of six or eight metres), this permitted development right is not automatic – one must apply for prior approval. For Class AA proposals, the council assesses the proposal on its design and its impact on neighbours. Since these are the two main issues in most householder planning applications, the new permitted development right does not really permit anything that would not otherwise be granted permission through a conventional planning application.

The new Class AA has been widely reported in the media as a "planning free for all", amid concerns that it will prompt a rash of monstrous new extensions in our suburbs. This is unlikely. Some commentators expected that, though councils would still be able to assess the design and impact on neighbours, they would take a "light touch" or permissive approach – it is supposed to be permitted development, after all. But it does not appear to be working out that way. Councils appear to have been refusing all the applications that come before them. It is too early to tell how the proposals will fare at appeal; at the time of writing, the first decisions have not yet come through (Just Planning has several such appeals pending) – but this bizarre new permitted development right will probably not be a silver bullet for homeowners hoping to extend towards the sky.

Other PD Rights

There are various other householder permitted development rights worth exploring. There are rights relating to paving a front garden (Class F), installing a chimney, vent or flue (Class G), installing a microwave antenna (Class H), and erecting boundary walls and fencing (Part 2, Class A). As explained earlier, the best way to get an understanding of all the permitted development rights is to the check out the government's "interactive house" website.

Danger: The Pitfalls of Householder PD Rights

Since the GPDO grants planning permission for householder development subject to various limitations, there is no need to apply for permission before starting work. However, this is risky. If, for any reason, your development is not in fact PD, the council will consider it to be unauthorised and you are at risk of enforcement action, with the possibility that it will have to be demolished. This is more common than you might expect. I will explain below how to obtain a Certificate of Lawfulness from the council to confirm that your proposed development is PD, but first let us explore why it might not be.

Representing homeowners who have built an extension in good faith, and then discovered that it is not permitted development and they may have to demolish it, is a big part of my caseload. It is a difficult and stressful situation for homeowners and best avoided. The following sections set out some of the key pitfalls to be aware of.

FAILING TO COMPLY WITH THE PD CRITERIA

The most common reason people run into enforcement problems when building an extension using their permitted development rights is that it does not quite comply with the specific requirements set out in the legislation. If your extension is deeper or taller than the limitations in the GPDO, for example, it is not permitted development and the entire structure will require planning permission.

By far the biggest issues arise in relation to rear dormer roof extensions. Class B allows very large rear box dormers. These are generally much larger than councils would give planning permission for, when a planning application is required. If, therefore, you have built a dormer that is not quite PD, the council is unlikely to grant retrospective planning permission and you face the horror of having to demolish it. This is a key point and a fundamental problem in the householder planning system, so allow me to repeat it: councils will not normally give you planning permission for a large dormer, so if you build one thinking it is PD, but make a small mistake that means that you have not met the PD requirements, you may have to demolish it.

Dormers – the Volume Limit and 20-Centimetre Trap

It is very easy to build a dormer that is not quite PD. Firstly, the designers who prepare plans do not always measure the roof properly. If they underestimate the height of the ridge (the very top of the roof), and the dormer is consequently built larger than shown on the plans, the extension may exceed the 40- or 50-cubic-metre volume allowance. It is also important to remember that the allowance is cumulative – it includes all previous roof alterations. If a previous owner built a rear extension many decades ago, the volume of the roof over their extension will be deducted from your cubic volume allowance for the dormer.

Secondly, builders – often with the tacit approval of the homeowner, but sometimes without the homeowner's knowledge – build something slightly larger in order to make maximum use of the roof space available. Sometimes the builder discovers that the roof is not quite high enough to create a new loft conversion with comfortable ceiling height. You need at least 2.1 metres for a usable room, but 2.4 metres is preferable. Remember that that the actual structure of the roof (timber joists and insulation) will reduce the internal height by a couple of hundred millimetres. If you can't achieve a comfortable height, the temptation is to slightly increase the height of the ridge, but a roof extension is not PD if the ridge is raised.

Thousands of homeowners do this every year, but if the council becomes aware of it you may find yourself in a sticky situation. It is difficult to tell from street level if your roof is tall enough to be comfortably converted, though experienced designers and builders can usually tell at a glance. If in doubt, take a look at your neighbours' roofs – dormer extensions are so popular these days that, if none of your neighbours have built one, it is likely the roofs on your street aren't tall enough.

Similarly, Class B requires that dormers be set back 20 centimetres from the edge of the roof. This is so there is a visual break between the rear wall of the house and the start of the new dormer and so that the dormer does not appear as a full new floor but as an extension. This frustrates builders, who see the 20 centimetres as a token setback and an unnecessary expense (it is cheaper and easier to build directly onto the rear wall). However, without the 20-centimetre setback, your extension is not PD. If the council never finds out, it will never be a problem, but if the **planning enforcement** team comes knocking, you may have to rebuild the rear wall of your new dormer.

In all honesty, few developments are built out exactly as shown on the approved drawings – projects evolve as building work takes place. There is some flexibility if you have obtained full planning permission through a planning application – if the alterations are minor and uncontroversial, the planners can approve a new application. The difficulty with PD is that there are no shades of grey. A development either meets the requirements and is PD, or doesn't, and isn't. If you create a development that is not permitted development under the specific limitations of the legislation, it is not authorised and, if a neighbour complains and the council gets involved, you may find yourself subject to enforcement action. In reality, most people get away with it, but an unlucky few don't and the consequences can be serious.

CASE STUDY: THE DORMER THAT ROSE SLIGHTLY ABOVE THE RIDGE

Claire owns a charming two-bedroom cottage close to the Thames in west London. She hired builders to convert her loft into an extra bedroom, adding a box dormer to the rear. The builders told her confidently that the development was permitted development and that she needn't contact the planners ("we have done dozens of these dormers around here, no need to worry"). When the works were finished, the roof of the new dormer was very slightly (100 millimetres or so) above the ridge – that is, it rose higher than the top of the original roof. Because Claire's house is terraced, you could just about see from the front that the roof line was not quite the same as the neighbours' (as shown in figure 15). The council visited and asked her to reduce the height or apply for planning permission for the development as built. She applied but was refused retrospective planning permission. She approached my colleagues and I at Just Planning and we successfully appealed the council's refusal.

The appeal inspector judged that the very slight difference in height was not especially visible from the street and dormers were a strongly established feature of the area, and that there was therefore no meaningful harm to its character or appearance.

Figure 15: Claire's increased roof height is visible from the street

THE "INTERPRETATION" OF PD RIGHTS

There is no real excuse for failing to comply with a clear and unambiguous requirement of the GPDO. However, a key failing of permitted development is that the legislation is difficult to understand. Even planning consultants and case officers struggle to answer the simplest questions: can I replace my timber window with uPVC? Can I install external insulation? Can I lay a patio? It is unsurprising that the rights are complicated – they cover all of England and all different housing types and individual situations – but ambiguity exposes homeowners to the risk of building something in good faith that is later found to be unlawful.

Sometimes the criteria themselves are vague. For most extensions, materials must be similar to those on the existing house. But how similar? If building a dormer roof extension, can you clad it in timber on the basis that your ground floor extension is clad in the same way? If you want a dormer clad in zinc, can you first add some zinc to some small part of the building and then claim that the new dormer cladding is a match? You cannot build an outbuilding forward of the main front wall of your house. But what if your house faces onto two streets (on a corner plot)?

Planning law says that these matters are the judgement of the decision-maker. In other words, the council case officer (or an appeal inspector, if a decision has been appealed) must interpret the GPDO as faithfully as possible. Appeal decisions are a form of case law – canny homeowners will always check with a planning consultant that the council's interpretation of PD rights is correct. If not, they should appeal the decision.

CASE STUDY: A HOUSE WITH TWO FACES

In 2018, Mrs Pointer applied to the London Borough of Hillingdon for confirmation that her proposed roof extensions were permitted development. She has a corner house, facing onto two roads (a main road and a side road) and understood that her roof extensions could only be built to the side and rear roof slopes, not on the front.

The council refused the application, agreeing that her extensions could only be on the side and rear roof slopes, but arguing that one of the extensions that she had proposed was actually on the front roof slope. Mrs Pointer was surprised by this decision; she certainly did not consider that part of her house to be the front – as far as she was concerned it was the side and faced onto a side road.

In any case, she decided not to argue and instead submitted a new application, moving her roof extensions to what the council had said it considered to be the side and rear roof slopes. The council refused this application as well, now arguing that the other street-facing roof slope should also considered to be the front of the house. The council had refused two applications, reaching different conclusions about what part of the roof should be considered to be facing the front.

We appealed both decisions on her behalf. The appeal inspector agreed with our interpretation of which elevation should be considered the front elevation of the property and awarded full costs against the council (i.e. required the council to compensate Mrs Pointer for the cost of appealing) for their unreasonable and contradictory decisions.

Situations in Which PD Rights Do Not Apply or Have Been Removed

The Flats v Houses Anomaly

The oddest anomaly in the householder planning system is that houses have permitted development rights, but flats do not. This means that, in a row of terraced properties, the houses may be extended in ways that converted flats in identical buildings right next door can only dream of.

A classic case is the dormer loft extension, whereby the rear roof of the building is squared off to provide another floor, as described earlier in this chapter. Householders can build large dormer roof extensions under permitted development. However, the same dormer extension to a house that has been converted into two flats is not PD. For flats, planning permission is always required and, if you submit an application, it is likely you will face stiff resistance from the council. Most councils have policies or guidance that limit the size of rear dormers – a very common requirement is that they take up less than half the roof and are set away from all sides, for example. Some councils rule out side dormers and hip-to-gable roof extensions altogether.

You may, however, be granted approval for a larger dormer if you can show that so many other buildings in the neighbourhood have been extended in this way that it has become a characteristic of the area. In other words, if lots of your neighbours (ideally next-door neighbours) have big dormer roof extensions, a larger dormer on your roof will not look out of place. Step 3 provides more information on how you might get planning permission for a development without complying with the council's planning polices and guidance.

REMOVAL OF PERMITTED DEVELOPMENT RIGHTS BY CONDITION

When councils grant planning permission, they may impose **conditions**. When granting permission for new houses, or large estates comprised of new houses, councils often impose a condition removing permitted development rights.

Most houses in England were built pre-war – there was no such thing as planning conditions when Victorian terraces were built. However, if your house was built in the post-war period (i.e. since 1945), it is possible that there is a planning condition (written on the decision notice for the planning approval) removing your permitted development rights. It is especially common with houses built since the 1970s.

This is often grossly unfair – why shouldn't new houses enjoy the same rights as all others? In some cases, it makes sense. If you are building a new house on a very small site, very close to neighbours, it may be appropriate that more control is exercised over how you extend in future. However, in the majority of cases it is not justified. The government's guidance states that conditions of this kind should only rarely be used and, if your house is affected by a condition of this kind, you can apply to have it removed. Just Planning successfully removes planning conditions like this for many clients each year.

If your house was built in the post-war period and you would like to take advantage of permitted development rights to extend, check first with the council whether these rights were removed when the house was granted planning permission.

CASE STUDY: SAMANTHA'S HOUSE HAD NO PERMITTED DEVELOPMENT RIGHTS AT ALL

Samantha Wilcox wanted to convert her loft space in order to add extra bedrooms to her family home. She took advice and was informed that she could take advantage of permitted development rights to replace her rear roof-slope with a large box dormer. She instructed builders and carried out the works. A few months after the works were completed, a planning enforcement officer knocked on her door. She lived in an estate that was built in the 1980s and, when permission was granted for the dozens of houses on that estate, permitted development rights were removed. She did not have a copy of this decision notice and had no idea that permitted development rights could be removed in this way. In retrospect, she had found it odd that very few other houses in her estate had rear dormers, despite their tall, capacious roofs.

With our help, Samantha applied to her local council for retrospective planning permission (i.e. for permission to keep the development as built). This application was refused and she was informed that the dormer must be removed in its entirety. We appealed the decision on her behalf and were delighted that the appeal was successful and planning permission was granted – the inspector concluded that the dormer was not easily seen from the street and integrated well with the house and its surroundings.

CONSERVATION AREAS AND ARTICLE 4 DIRECTIONS

If an area has special architectural or historic interest and its original character is well-preserved, the council can designate it as a **conservation area**. Every council area in England has at least one conservation area and there are now over 10,000 across the country. Conservation areas are subject to additional planning controls – it is much harder to get planning permission for new developments in conservation areas and though it is a privilege to live in a place recognised for its special qualities, homeowners should be aware of this downside.

Some permitted development rights, such as Class B roof extensions, do not apply in conservation areas (nor in the less common but equally important Areas of Outstanding Natural Beauty (AONB), the Broads, National Parks, and World Heritage Sites). In addition, councils have the right to suspend other PD rights if they feel that the extensions permitted by those rights would cause particular harm. They do this through the introduction of an **Article 4 Direction**. In many conservation areas, relatively minor developments like the erection of satellite dishes, the replacement of windows, and the repainting of exterior render need planning permission.

CASE STUDY: THE UNLAWFUL DORMER
IN A CONSERVATION AREA

Chris and his wife Heather bought a charming, two-bedroom, terraced house in a suburb of Birmingham in 2011. Chris is my mortgage broker and knows the mortgage market inside out. Though I bother him endlessly for free financial advice, he didn't drop me a line before deciding to extend his house with a large rear dormer roof extension. His builder told him it was permitted development (which, as we have seen, it usually is). The works were completed, and Chris and Heather were delighted with their new extension, which was the envy of the street (but, suspiciously, the only dormer of its kind in the area).

In 2016, the couple decided to sell. They came to me when their buyer's solicitor asked for evidence that the dormer had permission, pointing out that, since the house was in a conservation area, it did not have PD rights for roof extensions. It is unusual that solicitors are so well informed on planning matters, but this one had clearly done her homework. Happily, since the works had been carried out more than four years previously (see later in this chapter for more on the 4-year rule), the development was immune from enforcement action and I obtained a Certificate of Lawfulness from the local council to confirm that the development was now lawful by virtue of the passage of time. Simon and Heather are now happily ensconced in a larger house, with disaster averted and a lesson learnt (and the buyers of their old home still have the only dormer on the street!).

Other Unforced Errors

Don't Take Planning Advice from Your Builder

When homeowners run into enforcement problems with an extension they have already built, they often blame their builder. Builders have a lot of experience in householder extensions and a general idea of what kind of development is and is not permitted development under the regulations. But they cannot be expected to understand all of the various limitations (as outlined in this chapter). They will not have checked whether the homeowners' permitted development rights have been removed by condition or that the house is in a conservation area, for example. They cannot be expected to be familiar with all of the complexities of the householder planning system. Homeowners must do their own homework.

Don't Base Your Decisions on What Your Neighbour Has Built

It is dangerous and rash to assume that, if your neighbour has built something under PD, it follows that you may do the same. The neighbour's development may not be PD and it may just be a matter of time before the council takes an interest. Or they may miss your neighbour's development but target yours. If the neighbour's development is lawful, there may still be many reasons why the same development would not be PD on your house. You may be over the border in a conservation area, or your house may have a restrictive planning condition removing PD rights, or there may be site-specific circumstances (the design of your house and its relationship with its boundaries) that make an important difference.

Similarly, if none of your neighbours have carried out a particular form of development, it may be a sign. Dormer roof extensions are so common in general, that if there are none visible in your immediate area it is likely that this kind of extension is not permitted development (for one of the reasons I have given). It may also be simply that the lofts of the houses on your street are not tall or large enough to accommodate an extension without raising the height of the roof – which is never permitted development, and also difficult to get full planning permission for.

Don't Take a Council Planner's Word for It

A surprising number of clients facing enforcement action tell me that, "I called the council and one of the planners said it was ok." When I worked as a council planner, I often had those conversations with local residents. Typically, they would ask, "Can I build a rear extension under PD?" I would reply that, "yes, you can, but you are advised to prepare plans and submit an application to the council to confirm that your proposal complies." Unfortunately, a lot of people stop listening after "yes, you can".

I have very little sympathy with clients who tell me that the council said it was ok. It seems extraordinary that someone would spend tens of thousands of pounds on a development without a piece of paper in their hand to confirm that it was lawful. Permitted development regulations are complex – it is impossible for a planner to casually advise over the phone whether or not your development is lawful. They would need to check if you are in a conservation area, check if you are affected by planning conditions, make sure you live in a house and not a flat, check how your house has been extended in the past, and check that your specific proposals comply in every respect with the detailed requirements of the legislation. Planners are not bound by casual advice given outside a formal decision notice and the only way to be sure your development is lawful is to apply for a Certificate of Lawfulness.

Certificates of Lawfulness – Certainty That Your Development Is Lawful

There is only one way to be sure that your proposal is PD and that is to prepare a full set of plans (as you would if you were applying for full planning permission) and submit an application to the council for a Certificate of Lawfulness (also known as a "Lawful Development Certificate").

Whereas a planning application asks the council to decide whether a proposal complies with planning policies, a Certificate of Lawfulness application asks the council to confirm that a proposal is lawful in light of relevant legislation. This is written confirmation from the council that your proposed extensions are indeed permitted development and that you may proceed with the building work. It should *always* be obtained before starting work.

Applying for a Certificate of Lawfulness is pretty much the same as applying for planning permission. Choose a good designer (taking account of my tips in Step 1), prepare a short supporting statement that explains how the development complies with the relevant part of the GPDO, and submit a set of plans and the planning fee (which is set at 50 percent of the equivalent fee for a full planning application). Just as with a householder planning application, the case officer is likely to do a quick site visit and the decision will take around eight weeks. If the council makes a mistake in assessing your application but does issue a Certificate of Lawfulness (i.e. it issues a certificate on the mistaken belief that your development is PD), you may still proceed – the council is bound by its decision.

There is no obligation to apply for a certificate – if you are sure your proposal is permitted development, you may proceed. However, for the reasons I have given, this may be risky. In any case, apart from giving you comfort that your development is PD, the certificate also serves as confirmation for buyers, mortgage lenders, and their solicitors when you come to refinance or sell your home. As we have discussed, non-planners (and some planners) have a poor understanding of PD and a Certificate of Lawfulness is the only way to demonstrate conclusively that your development was lawful when you carried it out.

Beware of Combining PD Rights with Full Planning Consents

PD rights are generally more generous than what can be achieved under a full planning application, but they are strictly limited by the criteria set out by the GPDO. This creates dilemmas for applicants.

Take, for example, a situation where the council is willing to grant planning permission for a two-storey rear extension that is three metres deep on the ground floor and two metres deep on the first floor. For the homeowner, this would provide an enlarged kitchen/diner as well as an extra bedroom upstairs. On the other hand, using PD rights, the homeowner could extend to six metres on the ground floor (using the larger home extension scheme), double what the council would allow. However, this PD right applies to single-storey extensions only – they would not be able to build on top of their six-metre extension.

Some homeowners think they can solve this problem by obtaining permission for both developments and building them together. In other words, they obtain prior approval (under PD rights) for a six-metre-deep ground floor extension but also obtain full planning permission for a two-storey extension (three metres at ground floor and two metres at first floor) and then combine the best of both in a single structure – a two-storey extension that is six metres deep at ground floor and two metres at first floor.

I am frequently approached by clients who have taken this approach and run into planning enforcement problems. The six-metre extension under permitted development is only lawful if built on its own. The permission is for a single-storey extension and it must therefore be single-storey when built. Similarly, the two-storey extension is only lawful if it has a maximum depth of three metres at ground floor level. Building the best of both really means that the structure does not comply with either approval and is unlawful.

The solution is to obtain prior approval for a six-metre single-storey extension and build it, so that it is a lawfully-completed structure. Then (and only then) apply for a first floor two-metre-deep extension, showing the new six metre extension on the existing plans. As the ground floor element is existing and lawful, the council will focus on the first-floor addition only and should approve it on the basis that it is only two metres deep.

Step 4, on how to apply tactically and effectively, provides more advice on how to combine permitted development and planning applications and how to get around planning obstacles. Step 6, on planning enforcement, cautions further on the risks and consequences of carrying out development that is not strictly lawful.

CASE STUDY: THE HOUSE WITH THREE CONSENTS BUT NO PERMISSION

Pritam needed more room. His three kids were growing up and his mother-in-law had come to live with the family in their three-bedroom semi in Walsall. He had seen his neighbours build big extensions over the years, had saved up a good pot of money, and wanted to increase the size of his house substantially.

His designer knew that the council would not grant permission for a series of large extensions. Its planning guidance limited the width, height, and depth of new structures. So, he proposed applying for three separate permissions: prior approval (using permitted development rights) for a single-storey rear extension with a depth of six metres; full planning permission for a two-storey side and rear extension, and use standard permitted development rights (no application needed) for a rear dormer roof extension.

Pritam obtained the recommended permissions and set to work on this combination of extensions. He also built an outbuilding at the rear of the garden (which was permitted development). A neighbour complained to the council just as the extensions were being finished and a planning enforcement officer came on site to investigate. She explained to Pritam that it wasn't possible to build all of these structures at once – the single-storey, six metre extension was not lawful because it was built with a first floor element on top; the planning consent had not been implemented correctly because the ground floor was six metres rather than three metres deep, and the dormer was not permitted development because the side extensions had used up some of the 50 cubic metre volume allowance for roof extensions under the permitted development criteria. Only the outbuilding was lawful.

Pritam applied retrospectively for all of the extensions and was refused permission. The council served an enforcement notice requiring that the extensions be removed. I appealed the notice on Pritam's behalf and was very disappointed when the inspector dismissed the appeal, deciding that the extensions were too bulky and looked out of place. At the time of writing, we are negotiating with the council to see if some of Pritam's extensions can be saved from demolition. Pritam's experience is a cautionary tale – it is possible to combine permitted development rights and full planning approvals to create larger extensions, but always take professional advice to ensure that you don't run into enforcement problems.

What to Do if Your Proposal Is Not PD

I have explained that lots of properties do not have PD rights and that the rights can, in any case, be heavily circumscribed. They grant permission for specific, isolated developments and they are curtailed and limited. If you do not have permitted development rights, or you want to extend in ways that are not currently PD, you will need to apply for full planning permission. That presents its own challenges and complications. The next chapter will guide you through them.

STEP 2 SUMMARY

1. If you want to extend your home, you should start by exploring your permitted development (PD) rights. They allow you to carry out certain types of development without applying for full planning permission and generally permit larger extensions than local councils would usually allow.

2. However, PD rights are not always well understood. There are very strict limitations on how they may be used and it is very easy to come a cropper. The consequences of building something that is close to, but not quite, PD are severe: every year, homeowners across England (including clients of mine) have to demolish extensions they had built in good faith, just not in accordance with the rules.

3. This chapter has outlined the main pitfalls. The key point is to take professional advice (not casual advice from your builder or informal advice from a council planner) and to apply for a Certificate of Lawfulness – this is the only way you can be certain you are on the right track.

Step 3:
Understand How Planning Decisions Are Really Made

You have chosen a good local designer. You have established whether or not your house has permitted development rights, and have worked out that some or all of what you want to achieve needs full planning permission. So, now you will draw up plans. And you will apply. And you will wait for eight weeks. And you will be at the mercy of a creaky planning system and a cranky council planner.

According to planning law, decisions must be made in light of planning policies and any other material considerations (more on those later). In theory, then, the outcomes should be predictable and sensible proposals should sail through. Unfortunately, planning decision-making is not entirely predictable – some policies are loosely worded and case officers have considerable discretion. Most decisions are really a matter of experience and judgement. Since it is generally the most junior officers dealing with lowly householder applications, experience and judgement are not always in good supply.

Maximising your chances of getting approval is a two-step process. This chapter will help you understand how planning policies are applied and how exceptions to them can be justified. We will also explore the most common householder development types and the main planning considerations that apply to them (from the character of the area through to highways and more). The following chapter explores how you might influence the decision-making process to get the outcome you want.

Planning Policies and 'Other Material Considerations'

I have suggested that the planning decision-making process is random – with case officers deciding whether to grant approval depending on their mood. That is not, of course, strictly true. Planning law states that planning applications should be decided in accordance with planning policies. Those policies are published in a (relatively) easy to read format and are available on every council website. The policies are often supported by **supplementary planning documents**, which provide more detailed guidance on what kind of extensions may be granted permission.

An application for planning permission should not be a complete stab in the dark. You should have a pretty good idea of whether or not you will be granted permission before you apply. It is understandable that homeowners do not fully understand how planning applications are assessed. However, if you have found an agent who proposes submitting an application on your behalf but has no idea what the local policies are and cannot clearly explain how your proposal will assessed and why it is likely to be successful, you need to find better representation. Even if you are relying on the skills and knowledge of a trusted agent, it is a good idea for applicants to have a general knowledge of how planning decisions are made.

The Planning Policy Hierarchy

In England, there is a single (brief) document that provides the highest-level strategic policies. It is called the **National Planning Policy Framework (NPPF)** and it is worth a read, especially if you want a better understanding of how the planning system as a whole operates. However, it does not contain the detailed local policies that really determine whether or not you will be granted planning permission for a small-scale development.

For the London boroughs, there are citywide planning policies set out in the **London Plan**. The London Plan is a much longer and denser document, but its policies are also more strategic than local and not especially relevant to smaller (especially householder) applications.

The most important policies for smaller-scale planning applications are those set out in local planning documents, and these differ from council to council. To view yours, go to your council's website (usually councilname. gov.uk), click on "planning" and then "policies". You will be presented with a list of policy documents of various types. It may take time to work out which documents are relevant, but don't be daunted.

The Development Plan

The collection of policies affecting an area is known as the **development plan**. The plan will either be a single document or, more commonly, be split into two main documents: one setting out more strategic, higher-level objectives (new housing, a healthy environment, economic growth) and the other providing specific policies (good design, prevention of harm to neighbours, specific parking standards).

For no good reason, there is no uniform naming system for these documents. Some councils simply call them the **local plan**. The more strategic document is often called the **core strategy** or the "strategic policies". The specific policies document is often called **development management policies**. There will also be a "proposals map": a map of the area showing

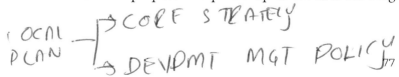

geographic restrictions, such as the extent of the green belt or the boundaries of conservation areas.

In England, smaller areas now have the power to draw up **neighbourhood plans**, which may have policies of their own. Finally, local authorities can introduce additional guidance in the form of supplementary planning documents (SPDs), which are specific to a certain area or type of development. SPDs commonly provide specific and detailed guidance on householder extensions and on smaller property developments.

To work out what policies and guidance apply to householder extensions, for example, read the local policies applied to individual planning applications (usually called the local plan or development management policies) and check if your council has supplementary guidance (an SPD) specifically relating to householder extensions.

Figure 16: The planning policy Hierarchy

The government and local councils pay lip service to community involvement and public participation, but they don't make it easy. Council websites are clunky and planning documents are full of jargon. The jargon makes planners and planning consultants feel important, but it serves the public very poorly.

If you have trouble establishing what the relevant local policies and guidance are, try calling the planning department – most have a **duty planning service** whereby a planner will be on duty and will provide general advice. Simply ask for a list of policies relating to householder developments and for general information on what they mean and how they are applied.

A shortcut to understanding the council's policies for extensions and other householder developments is to find a similar application that has been decided recently in your area. All planning authorities have a database of planning applications on their website and you can search by keyword or generate a list of all applications decided in recent weeks.

If you identify an application that looks similar to what you are proposing, click through the associated documents and look for the officer's report (sometimes known as the "delegated report"), a detailed report prepared by the case officer that describes the site and the proposal, lists the relevant planning policies and then assesses the proposal in light of these policies. Take a look at several different proposals to see what issues reappear. A small number of councils do not upload officers' reports to their websites, but they are nevertheless public documents, so contact the planning department for a copy.

It stands to reason that reading the detailed assessments of similar applications will help you decide if yours is likely to find favour. Officers' reports are a platinum planning resource and too few applicants ever read them. Many architects and planning agents are also ignorant of how they shed light on a council's approach to various planning issues. For planning consultants, officers' reports are the single most useful tool for getting a sense of how planning applications are decided for a particular type of development in a particular area.

OTHER MATERIAL CONSIDERATIONS

At the beginning of this chapter, I said that planning law requires planning decisions to be made strictly in accordance with the development plan (i.e. the planning policies). However, this is not the full story. Decisions must be made in accordance with the development plan *unless* **other material considerations** indicate otherwise.

A material consideration is something that must be taken into account when determining a planning application. It is a very important concept in planning and is at the heart of all decision-making. As discussed above, planning policies are the most obvious, and perhaps the most important, material considerations. But there are other considerations that may affect a decision, such as:

- any supplementary planning documents (SPDs) that have been adopted;
- the extent to which the council's policies are up to date and accord with national policy;
- emerging policies that have not yet been adopted;
- the planning history of the site – for example, if permission has already been granted for something similar;
- the physical context – the siting and design of the existing building and its neighbours.

There are some things that cannot be considered material considerations, such as:

- loss of value to an individual property;
- loss of a private individual's view;
- legal property issues, such as boundary disputes or the ownership of land; and,
- the applicant's personal character or motivation in applying (their alleged greed, for example).

THE PLANNING BALANCE

When assessing an application, case officers should balance the competing material considerations, judging their relative importance. In well-written reports or appeal decisions, you will see the officer consider each of the considerations in turn and attach a weight to them.

Greater weight will be attached to some considerations. A decision-maker will take a dim view of proposals that are in direct conflict with clear, unambiguous, up-to-date planning policies. They will place a lot of weight on perceived harm to a neighbour's living conditions and harm to the character of the street (especially harm to listed buildings and other heritage assets).

The decision-maker will then consider whether there are any other material considerations that outweigh any harm that has been identified. They might decide, for example, that possible harm to a neighbour's living conditions is mitigated (resolved, in this context) by requiring that a window that would overlook the neighbour be obscure-glazed (that, is, installed with frosted glass). Conflict with a planning policy might be justified by site-specific circumstances – such as the fact that a neighbour has built something very similar (see later in this chapter for more on precedent). A proposal for new housing might be allowed on the basis that the area is suffering a severe housing shortage, even if there is some harm to the character of the area, for example.

WHY DO CASE OFFICERS FAIL TO FIND THE PLANNING BALANCE?

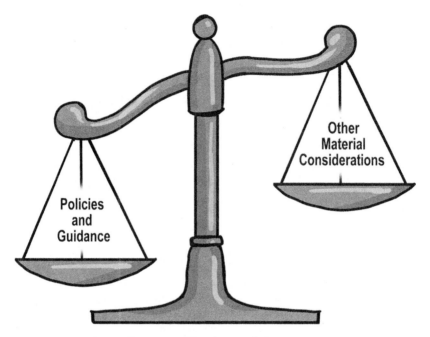

Figure 17: The planning balance

One of the things that strikes me about some case officers (and I say this having been one myself) is their lack of confidence in decision-making. It may be because their recommendations must pass through a senior officer and it is generally best to be uncontroversial. It might be the product of working in a bureaucratic system where process is valued over innovation. Many planners think that they are holding back a tidal wave of bad design and must not give an inch. Whatever it is, they tend not to stick their necks out. Their first instinct is to refuse anything that does not strictly comply with adopted policies and guidance. When they consider the planning balance, they place much more emphasis on the policies and guidance than on other material considerations.

Planning policies are the starting point, but other material considerations are just as important. Every site is unique: it is large or small, differs in proximity to its neighbours, is orientated in a different direction to other buildings and has its own individual character. Planning policies and supplementary guidance cannot cover every eventuality – some flexibility must be shown.

Guidance limiting rear extensions to three metres may be appropriate for most houses, but not for one where both of its neighbours have already extended to four metres, for example, or where the neighbouring houses are some distance away. Guidance setting side extensions back from the front wall of the house might make sense in most cases, but not where the architectural design of the house means that a setback of this kind would look out of place. Guidance that extensions be finished with pitched (i.e. sloping) roofs should not apply in areas where pitched roofs are not very common. One might look past guidance discouraging roof terraces if a terrace is tucked away from view and designed so that there is no direct overlooking of neighbours' gardens.

The problem is that case officers are reluctant to acknowledge these exceptions to their precious rules. As a result, some designers advise their clients not even to apply. Or homeowners apply, get refused, and give up. Perfectly good proposals get refused again and again because they don't comply with rules that shouldn't apply to them. One of the reasons I left council planning and began working for homeowners as a planning consultant is because I saw how often they were getting a raw deal.

CASE STUDY: A FOUR-METRE-DEEP REAR EXTENSION IN LIVERPOOL

Mrs Ling was told by her council that their guidance limits the depth of single-storey rear extensions to three metres, on the basis that a greater depth would look oversized and would overshadow the neighbours. However, her architect had told her that a four-metre-deep extension was the best design solution for her house. It would sit alongside an existing kitchen extension (which could be opened up internally) and would look strange if it stopped one metre short of the back wall.

Exasperated, and unsure of what to do, she came to Just Planning for advice. When we examined the plans and some satellite images, we saw that there was a three-metre-high brick wall between her house and the closest neighbouring property. So, there was no way that a deeper extension would overshadow that neighbour. We agreed with her architect that a four-metre-deep extension (aligning with the kitchen) made much more sense – a three metre extension would have looked odd.

We recommended to Mrs Ling that she submit an application against the council's advice. Just Planning wrote a detailed Supporting Statement acknowledging the guidance but explaining which other material considerations justified a grant of planning permission in this case. Planning permission was duly granted, and Mrs Ling is now very happy with her new, enlarged and well-designed kitchen extension.

HOW PLANNING APPLICATIONS ARE ASSESSED IN PRACTICE

The previous sections explained that planning policies should be made in accordance with planning policies and any other material considerations. It also explained that the role of the case officer (or other decision-maker) is to weigh up all of the relevant considerations in the planning balance. Finally, it argued that case officers are not always very good at coming to a nuanced decision and often stick rigidly to policy requirements, discounting other important factors. We will now explore how planning applications are assessed in practice – what typical policies and guidance say and what other considerations come into play for householder developments (extensions).

The starting point for the assessment of most smaller-scale planning applications is *design and appearance* and the *impact on neighbours*. There are a host of other possible issues (such as parking, flood risk, or harm to a protected tree), but design and impact on neighbours are usually the two biggest issues; they are the twin pillars of the householder planning system.

The difficulty with both is that they are not very easy to assess. Design (whether a development harms the streetscene) is subjective – one person's

① Design + Apprnce
② Impact on NRs

castle is another person's eyesore – and case officers don't normally have any specific architectural or design training and can be allergic to anything unusual, adventurous or out of the ordinary.

Similarly, it is hard to be sure whether an extension or new building might overshadow a neighbour's windows or garden. Most extensions will have some impact on the neighbours but at what point does the impact become unacceptable?

Of course, no one wants to build something that blights the streetscene or plunges their neighbour's dining room into darkness. Some applicants need to be saved from themselves – many refusals are for terrible proposals and the case officer's intervention forces the applicant and their designer to think again, ultimately resulting in a much better proposal. The following sections will give you an idea of how planners think about the main planning issues, with examples of how policies are typically worded and what other considerations come into play.

THE CHARACTER OF THE AREA

Every council will have policies to say that a development should, for example, "represent high quality design", "respect and reflect the character of the surrounding area" and "reinforce local distinctiveness". Extensions should be proportionate in size and scale and use appropriate materials, and new dwellings should be similar to neighbouring houses. These kinds of policies are fairly generic – it is difficult to be specific about how development, in general, should be designed in order to protect the character and appearance of the area.

It is a core planning principle that any new development fits in with its immediate surroundings. To some degree, it is a matter of common sense. Huge extensions that overwhelm the original house and look out of place when viewed from the street are not going to be approved. You can leave the detailed design of the proposal to a good designer, but it's useful to know how to "read" the surrounding area to understand what might be appropriate.

Streets Characterised by Uniformity

Along most streets, the building plots are roughly the same size and the houses on them are similar in terms of height, depth, and width. They are usually laid out in a line (the "building line") and there is a distinctive architectural style. Any new structure must take account of this existing pattern of development.

Some streets have a particularly uniform character. Imagine a row of Victorian terraced houses, all identical with matching detailing and stretching into the distance in a regimented line. Now imagine a huge front dormer or a large porch to one of these houses. It would immediately stick out and be in conflict with the rhythm and pattern of development along the street. In figure 18, for example, the extension that sticks up at roof level looks out of place – none of the neighbouring houses have a development of this kind.

Figure 18: On a row of matching houses, an extension to one can look out of place

---

CASE STUDY: SIX PORCHES IN NEWHAM

In 2017, Newham Council issued enforcement notices to six houses on Norfolk Road. An enforcement notice is a formal legal document demanding that a breach of planning permission be reversed (that an extension that has been built without planning permission be demolished, for example). The notices alleged that the owners of these houses had built front porches without planning permission and that they must be demolished (porches can be permitted development, but the developments in question exceeded the PD limits).

In the council's view, the porches interrupted the clean lines of the terraced rows. The owners came together and instructed Just Planning to appeal the enforcement notices. Though we did our best to show that hundreds of similar Victorian houses in Newham had porches of this kind, the appeal inspector dismissed this argument (of precedent) and took the view that the porch additions harmed the streetscene and must be removed.

The inspector's reasoning was essentially that there is a uniformity to a Victorian terraced row – a repeating pattern of houses with matching bay windows and other architectural elements – and though porches had sprung up in the area, they nevertheless interrupted the pattern of development and looked out of place.

Streets with a Diverse Pattern of Development

Some streets are a jumble of different types of buildings. They differ in size (detached, terraced, blocks of flats, bungalows, three-storey townhouses), design (Victorian, post-war, contemporary), use (houses, flats, shops, offices, factories), materials (brick, timber, render, zinc), and architectural detailing (bay windows, flat roofs, integral garages). Many of the buildings may already have been altered and extended in lots of different ways, creating a diverse streetscene. In the example in figure 19, there is variation in the height and width of individual properties, a mishmash of architectural styles and a stepped building line. It is much easier to get planning permission on streets like this.

Figure 19: It is easier to extend houses on a mixed streetscene

For extensions, councils often have fairly prescriptive supplementary planning guidance. For example, it may recommend that side extensions be set back from the front wall of the house, so that there is a clear distinction between the old and the new. This is a valid aim. However, if the house next door to you has been extended to the side without a setback, your extension would look more out of place if you complied with the guidance than if you tried to harmonise with what your neighbour had already done.

Because case officers tend to take a cautious approach to applications, sometimes refusing anything that does not strictly comply with the guidance, it is important to make clear to them why you consider the neighbour's extension to be an important material consideration. Get your designer to show the neighbour's extension on your plans and highlight the fact that yours has been designed to harmonise with it. Include a brief Supporting Statement that acknowledges the guidance (to show that you are not ignorant of it or wilfully ignoring it) but argue that it is outweighed by another material consideration.

If that fails, and the council still refuses permission, read the decision notice and officer's report to try and understand why. Do they provide a robust response to your arguments? If you think you have a case, it important to appeal the decision – more on that in Step 5.

One last point – the character of the area is the area immediately around your property. A slew of similar extensions three streets away will not justify a similar proposal at your site. If you are arguing that your proposed development fits in with the surrounding pattern of development, you must identify properties visible from your house, i.e. buildings that are part of the immediate context.

CASE STUDY: A CROWD OF DORMERS IN NORTHAMPTON

In 2019, Brendan Michaels was refused planning permission for a rear dormer roof extension to his Victorian terraced house. The council said that the proposed dormer would be visible from a side street and was much larger than their published householder planning guidelines allowed. He approached Just Planning for help. When we looked at satellite images of the area, we could see that his was the only house in a row of five that had not extended to the rear at roof level, as shown in figure 20. Zooming out slightly, we discovered that, of the 14 houses closest to the application property, 11 had built full-sized rear dormer roof extensions. We appealed against the council's decision and were delighted to win the appeal.

Figure 20: Almost all of Brendan's neighbours already had roof extensions

The inspector decided that the proposed dormer was large, replacing the entire rear roof slope, and did not comply with the council's supplementary guidance on the size and siting of this kind of householder development. However, the large number of similar dormers on neighbouring houses had changed the character of the area sufficiently that the proposal would not look oversized or out of place and would fit in well with its surroundings. This is an example of other material considerations overcoming clear guidance against dormer extensions of this type and is evidence that case officers are biased towards planning policies and guidance, and away from other mitigating factors.

Subordination

The idea of **subordination** comes up again and again in the assessment of householder extensions. Essentially it means that an extension should be much smaller than the main house.

All houses have an original architectural design. Their size and layout are deliberate. Alterations can conflict with the architect's original intentions and can interfere with the proportions, balance, and symmetry of the building. If you have selected a good designer, they will take this into account when designing your extension. The challenge is that homeowners want to maximise the floor area of their new extension. They are willing to sacrifice design quality for more space. Applications for extensions are mostly commonly refused for the simple reason that they are just too *big*, and the size either represents poor design or harms the neighbours.

Planners therefore emphasise subordination. Planning policies and guidance recommend that extensions be subordinate to the host dwelling. The original building should remain the key architectural feature.

A single-storey extension will usually be subordinate to a two-storey house, but not if the extension has a floor area much larger than the footprint of the house. A side extension that is, say, 50 percent of the width of the main house may appear subordinate, but a side extension that doubles the width of the house may not be considered subordinate. A two-storey extension that is the same height as the existing house is probably not subordinate – lowering the roof form may help it sit more comfortably next to the original building.

THE IMPACT ON NEIGHBOURS

Decision-makers naturally place great importance on protecting residents from harmful development on neighbouring sites. Unfortunately, planning policies regarding this are also quite generic. They will require that development "causes no harm to neighbours in terms of a loss of light, outlook, privacy or general amenity", for example, without really explaining how the nature of any likely harm could be established. It comes as a surprise to clients that there is no simple, clear way in which these things are assessed – it is a matter of judgement.

In built up areas, where houses are packed cheek by jowl, new developments can obviously have an impact on close neighbours. Most houses line up side-by-side, with front and rear gardens similarly aligned. If you extend to the rear along both boundaries, that extension will probably be visible from your neighbours' rear windows and gardens.

If the houses are not neatly aligned, i.e. if your house is set at an angle to your neighbours, any harmful impact might be heightened. If you have a short garden with neighbours very close to the rear, any development will be immediately apparent from their side of the fence.

But being able to see a new structure is not the same as suffering an unacceptably harmful impact from it. At what point does a development cross the line? Broadly speaking, development can cause harm in terms of:

- a loss of light;
- a loss of outlook;
- overlooking/a loss of privacy;
- an overbearing impact/sense of enclosure.

This list is not exhaustive – a proposed roof terrace may also cause harm in terms of noise and disturbance when people sit outside, for example – but covers most of the concerns case officers raise. It is not expected that extensions will cause no harm at all, rather that they don't cause "unacceptable" harm. What is unacceptable harm? Good question.

Most councils have some kind of guidance for extensions (often published as a supplementary planning document [SPD]). These provide rules of thumb for the assessment of development proposals. It is common to limit the height and depth of single-storey rear extensions to three metres, for example, on the basis that a greater height and depth would lead to a loss of light and be overbearing.

Councils also commonly apply the 45-degree rule, whereby an imaginary line is drawn at a 45-degree angle from the midpoint of the nearest habitable window at the neighbour's property, as shown in figure 21. If your proposed extension crosses the 45-degree line, it is considered likely that it would reduce light levels to that window.

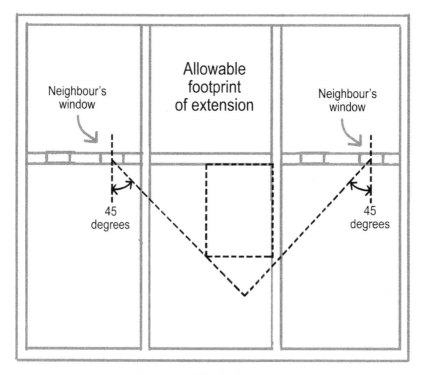

Figure 21: The 45-degree rule

For two-storey extensions projecting towards a neighbour, councils generally set a minimum separation distance between the extension you want to build and the closest neighbour. If the windows in your extension face windows in a neighbour's property, the minimum separation distance will be greater than if the windows in one house are facing a wall without windows (a side wall, say) in another.

Must you comply with the minimum separation distances at all times? Here, other material considerations may come into play. A row of tall trees along the boundary between the two houses may mean there is no possible overlooking or other harmful impacts, for example.

Apart from these crude measures, case officers are simply expected to reach their own judgement. This is one of the reasons the planning process is so uncertain, and it is difficult to be sure what will and will not be granted permission. There is no simple set of rules that can be applied directly and fairly to every house in every circumstance. Which is why you must take extra care to make your case as effectively as possible.

Clear, accurate plans help give the impression that the scheme has been sensitively designed (which is why I emphasise the importance of choosing the right designer in Step 1). An absence of neighbour objections also helps: if the case officer is sitting on the fence, and the neighbours don't seem to be concerned, they may be more inclined to grant approval. It also helps to have a good Supporting Statement making the case for the proposal. These aspects are considered a little more in later sections.

There are a few things to keep in mind that will help your case:

1. If the council is arguing that your development will lead to a loss of light affecting your neighbours, consider whether this is likely in practice. If your neighbour's garden faces directly south, for example, it will enjoy direct sunlight throughout most of the day. If it faces north, the garden may be overshadowed by the main houses themselves and your single-storey rear extension will not cast its own shadow.

2. Consider whether your neighbour has an extension of their own. Take a look at the boundary walls and fences – if there is a 2.5-metre-tall fence along the boundary between the two houses, your three-metre-tall extension will arguably not have a major impact. If your neighbour's house sits on slightly higher land than yours, the impact of your extension may be limited.

3. Consider what parts of the neighbour's property may be affected. Is it a little-used area of the garden, or the area they use most commonly for sitting out? Does the nearest window serve a 'habitable' room, i.e. a living room, bedroom, or dining room, or is it a (less important) 'non-habitable' room, such as a small kitchen, bathroom or utility room? Is it a secondary window to a better source of light in another elevation?

The sketch in figure 22 illustrates some of the other material considerations that may weigh in favour of a proposed single-storey rear extension, even if the extension is a little deeper than the council would usually allow.

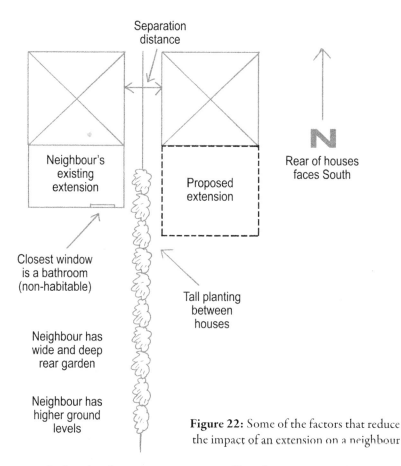

Figure 22: Some of the factors that reduce the impact of an extension on a neighbour

These are the kinds of arguments presented by planning consultants when making the case for a proposal. You can become more familiar with how these considerations are applied by reading the officers' reports (see earlier in this chapter for more on this priceless planning resource) for similar applications in your area where case officers have had to grapple with these issues.

Clients are often incredulous that planning assessments are not based on hard science. Most assessments are just a matter of judgement and experience.

The possible impacts are intangible – who is to say whether a neighbour will find a development overbearing upon them? If it is overbearing, will reducing its height or depth by 0.5 metres (say) eliminate the problem? What about moving it off the boundary by 200 millimetres? Clients find it intensely frustrating that planners don't have the answers to these questions.

The most important lesson here is that planning decision-making is not an exact science; it is not enough to simply submit an application and hope the case officer reaches the right decision. There are strong incentives for the officer to refuse permission – why take a risk if there is a possibility that harm will be eaused? – so it is important to prepare and manage your application in a way that maximises your chances of success.

QUALITY OF LIVING ACCOMMODATION

Applications for householder extensions sometimes run into difficulties around quality of accommodation, i.e. whether the house itself will still be bright and comfortable after the extension is built. Councils have been known to refuse applications for single-storey rear extensions where they would reduce natural light levels reaching the middle part of the house. Some councils insist (either in their policies or supplementary planning documents) that, when an existing house is extended, a specified minimum garden area is retained.

It seems unfair to me that an application for an extension should be resisted on this basis – if it is acceptable in terms of its design and appearance and does not cause any harm to the neighbours, it is up to the homeowners how much natural light they want in their own rooms and how much of their garden they are willing to sacrifice in order to accommodate the extension. If their priority is a large, bright breakfast room and they are happy with a dark internal playroom or a small patio garden, who is to say that this is not a valid choice? We have a high success rate when we take these kinds of refusals to appeal.

Highways and Parking

Some councils will not grant permission for householder extensions where the proposal increases the number of bedrooms and the existing number of off-street parking spaces is not thought to be sufficient for the likely numbers of residents in the enlarged house. For example, if you have a three-bedroom house and two parking spaces, and apply for a loft extension to create a fourth bedroom, the case officer may look at the local parking standards, note that four-bedroom houses should usually have three parking spaces (for example) and refuse permission.

This is an unreasonable position. Entirely new houses may cause parking problems, but it is not likely that householder extensions will make a real difference to parking in the local area. Although a proposal may increase the number of bedrooms, this is likely so that the family's children have more space (a room each), rather than to allow more adults with cars to move in. This is a good example of how the householder planning system can make excessive, unreasonable demands of homeowners applying for minor and uncontroversial extensions to their homes. Refusals of permission for householder extensions on parking grounds alone are often overturned on appeal.

Flood Risk

Flood risk, protected trees, and ecology can sometimes be issues. The Environment Agency identifies areas of land that are at particularly high risk of flooding from rivers or the sea, and councils may have local maps of flood risk from surface water or sewers. You can check whether you are in a flood zone on the Environment Agency's website (https://flood-warning-information.service.gov.uk/long-term-flood-risk). Applications for new residential development in Flood Zones 2 and 3 must be accompanied by a **Flood Risk Assessment (FRA)**.

When it comes to flood risk, extensions are less controversial than entirely new homes. They are usually small in scale and do not place more people in harm's way (an enlarged kitchen does not translate to more occupiers) but, in some cases, the council will still require that a full FRA is prepared and submitted. These can be expensive, so check with a planning consultant whether a requirement for an FRA is proportionate to the scale of the development being proposed.

PROTECTED TREES

Planning permission is not normally required for the removal, topping or lopping of a tree. However, all trees in conservation areas are protected. Outside conservation areas, the council can protect individual trees or groups of trees through a **Tree Preservation Order (TPO)**. Councils will serve TPOs on trees that have "amenity value", i.e. they make an important contribution to the character and appearance of the area. Wilful damage to a protected tree is a criminal offence. If you are in a conservation area or there are protected trees on or near your site, you will need permission from the council for any works to them. If your extension may have an impact on a protected tree, the council will expect you to instruct a specialist to prepare a tree survey and a method statement detailing how the building works will not cause harm to the tree.

The council may refuse planning permission for developments that are close to a protected tree and could harm the tree's root system or increase pressure in future for the tree to be removed. Councils have been known to serve TPOs on trees after an application is submitted, so applicants often carry out works to unprotected trees on the site prior to submitting their application (usually to the horror of objecting neighbours).

THE NATIONAL OBSESSION WITH GREEN BELTS AND CONSERVATION AREAS

Generally speaking, the government takes a more relaxed approach to smaller-scale developments than local councils do. The government created permitted development rights to (try and) liberate homeowners and developers from much planning control and, at appeal, the government's appeal inspectors take a fairly flexible approach to decision-making when they are determining planning appeals. However, the government has two obsessions that frustrate the ambitions of thousands of applicants every year: protection of the green belt, and protection of properties in conservation areas.

Green Belt

Green belts were created after the Second World War. The Town and Country Planning Act 1947 (the same piece of legislation that first introduced permitted development rights) allowed local authorities to designate doughnut-shaped tracts of land around their settlements as areas that should not be developed. The purpose of green belt land is to prevent towns from sprawling outwards and eventually merging into each other. Green belts encourage development to take place within the town boundaries. The key quality of green belts is their *openness*.

The general population has a fear that uncontrolled development will eventually pave over the countryside. As a result, and without reflecting on it to any great extent, voters are keen to preserve the green belt and politicians are generally loathe to interfere with it, despite a desperate need, nationwide, to build more houses.

The NPPF (the national planning policy document mentioned at the beginning of this chapter) says that new developments in the green belt must not be allowed, with limited exceptions. One exception is building "infill dwellings" in existing villages. An infill dwelling is essentially a house built to occupy a gap in the streetscene. Another is the replacement of existing buildings with a new development, where the new development is not much larger than the existing and does not have a greater impact on the openness of the green belt. This allows the demolition of existing houses and their replacement with new, slightly larger, dwellings, or sometimes the demolition of other buildings (such as outbuildings, or commercial buildings) in favour of new dwellings of a similar height and footprint.

People are often surprised to hear that limits on new development in the green belt also apply to householder extensions. The extension of a house is only allowed where the extension is not "disproportionate" to the original dwelling. In other words, if your house is in the green belt, you may extend it only in a modest or limited way. Crucially, all extensions carried out since the house was built must be taken into account so, if you have bought a house that was previously extended in the 1980s or 1990s for example, it is possible that you will not be able to extend it any further. Not all buyers are aware of this when they buy a home and it can be a source of great frustration.

The NPPF does not explain what it means by "disproportionate". In the planning policy hierarchy (explained earlier in this chapter), national policies set out a general strategic direction and it is up to local councils to add flesh to the bones through their own development plans. Some councils don't really define "disproportionate" either and it is down to individual planners to make a judgement on a case-by-case basis. That is clearly not good planning – how are applicants and their architects supposed to come up with an acceptable scheme with no direction whatsoever?

Most councils have some kind of specific guidance. It is common, for example, for councils to have a policy that says something like: "cumulative extensions (i.e. all previous extensions plus the development proposed) should not increase the floor area (or volume) of the original house by more than 40 percent."

Clearly, if you exceed this policy limit, you will need to justify it. For something like this, you will need the help of a planning consultant. When I advise clients on extensions in the green belt, I first work with their designer to establish how much the house has been extended in the past. Sometimes we discover that the house has already been extended beyond the percentage limit set out in policy. I check how dated the policy is and whether it is clear and unambiguously worded. I look at recent decisions in the council area for other extensions in the green belt to see how case officers have made their assessments (always read the officer's report!) and I check appeal decisions to see whether the council's refusals are standing up at appeal. If the policy is badly worded or out of date, if the council's own case officers don't pay much attention to it when making assessments or if they often refuse permission but then lose at appeal, I will generally advise the client to submit an application in contravention of the policy with a strategy of persuading the case officer to grant approval or of winning a subsequent appeal.

Apart from the simple mechanics of how far the extension increases the volume or floor area of the house, decision-makers will assess the extent to which a development reduces openness – the key characteristic of the green belt. Basement extensions, infill extensions to the rear and extensions that make use of the existing volume in the roof space, for example, all reduce openness less than a two-storey side extension might do, for example. The character of the surrounding green belt also matters. Much of the green belt is not very open at all – it "washes over" small settlements where, in some cases, the houses are so densely packed, the immediate area resembles the suburbs of a large town. In cases like that, it may be easier to persuade a case officer or appeal inspector that the proposed development will not reduce the openness of the surrounding green belt.

It is worth noting that houses in the green belt have the same permitted development rights as houses that aren't in a green belt. So, if you are unable to extend your house through a grant of planning permission (because your house has been extended in the past or the council considers your proposed extensions disproportionate to the original building), you should explore what can be built under your permitted development rights (see Step 2 for more on these rights).

We sometimes apply for Certificates of Lawfulness on behalf of clients to establish that they can add a certain quantum of floorspace under permitted development and then use this fallback position as a basis of negotiations with the planners to try and achieve the development the clients really want. As I will explain later in this chapter, fallback positions are a material consideration and if planners believe that the applicants will build out the alternative proposal, they may grant permission for something similar that does not cause greater harm in planning terms.

Conservation Areas

Conservation areas are areas designated by local councils as having special architectural or historic value; they are heritage assets, similar to listed buildings. Listed buildings are individual buildings of some importance; conservation areas are whole areas that have heritage value. They are usually older neighbourhoods with a strong street pattern and high-quality housing. The number of conservation areas has been expanding over time and every council in England has at least one. Some councils have a very large number of conservation areas and there are more than 10,000 in England as a whole.

Conservation areas have stronger planning controls. This is good news if you are a local resident who worries that your neighbours might build big, ugly extensions but bad news if you are expecting another child and are in sore need of a fourth bedroom or like the idea of a much larger kitchen.

The general idea is that the character and appearance of a conservation area should not evolve and change in the way that other streets will over time. Research has suggested that house prices are higher in conservation areas and that people generally value them, but many residents do not fully appreciate the limitations that apply when trying to extend their homes.

To begin with, some permitted development rights – such as the ability to make alterations at roof level – do not apply in conservation areas. Councils also have the power to remove specific permitted development rights, which they do by issuing an Article 4 Direction. It is common, for example, to remove the right to build a front porch or replace windows without having to apply for planning permission. In some conservation areas, residents do not even have the right to repaint their homes without seeking planning permission.

When a homeowner does apply for permission, the policy hurdles are higher. Outside a conservation area, permission will be granted as long as a development does not cause *unacceptable* harm to the character of the area. In a conservation area, all harm is considered unacceptable. In other words, permission will normally only be granted for developments that do not harm in any way the particular features of that conservation area that make it worthy of preservation.

This is true even of developments at the rear of houses, which are not visible from the street. Many Victorian terraced houses have outriggers: a rear projection with room along one side (the **side return**). Many homeowners extend the outrigger to the side to enlarge a narrow kitchen. Though these are normally relatively uncontroversial because they are hidden away at the back, councils may object that the extension interferes with the repeating pattern of outrigger and side returns along the terraced row, and therefore harms the original character of the conservation area.

If you are proposing a development in a **conservation area**, you must pay particular attention to my advice in Step 1 about choosing a good designer. High quality design will ease the passage of an application for an extension in a conservation area. Try to choose a designer with an understanding of conservation areas and older buildings.

When preparing an application, it is important to understand (and demonstrate to the local planners that you understand) what it is about this conservation area that gives it its special character and how your proposal takes this into account. In most cases, councils prepare a **character appraisal** that sets out the history of the area, why it has been designated and what is particularly worthy of preservation. The best character appraisals set out very clearly for applicants what the council is committed to protecting (sash windows, for example, or unbroken roof lines, or the gaps between neighbouring houses). If you understand what the council is trying to achieve, it is much easier to judge whether what you are proposing will find favour. The services of a good planning consultant can be invaluable here.

Listed Buildings

Conservation areas are not the only heritage assets to be aware of. Some buildings are **listed** for their historic significance – it is very hard to get permission for alterations to a listed building and your first call should be a heritage specialist. Historic England maintains an online database of listed buildings (historicengland.org.uk/listing/the-list), with information on the history of the building and any special features worthy of preservation.

Some buildings are "locally listed". Locally listed buildings are not listed at a national level but are considered important enough by the council to be given some extra protection. Around half of all councils in England have locally listed buildings and the heritage significance of the building will be assessed if a planning application is submitted.

OTHER SPECIAL DESIGNATIONS

Councils can designate **areas of special character**. These are areas that are not special enough to be designated as conservation areas (and thus enjoy the extra national planning protections that come with such a designation) but are nevertheless identified by the council as having some townscape, architectural, or landscape value that is worth protecting. If your house is in an area of special character, you will please the planners by looking up why the designation was made (i.e. what the council perceives this special character to be) and writing a line or two in your Supporting Statement to explain that your proposal respects and preserves this character.

Note also that National Parks, Areas of Outstanding Natural Beauty, and the Norfolk and Suffolk Broads are designated in recognition of their landscape qualities and natural beauty. They are sensitive to new development and therefore enjoy stricter planning controls and limits on permitted development rights.

THE PLANNING HISTORY

When assessing an application, the case officer must take the planning history into account. There is an expectation, if not a strict legal obligation, for decisions to be consistent with earlier decisions for similar proposals on the same site. Officers should only deviate from an earlier decision if the context has changed – if other developments have been carried out nearby, for example, or if the council has adopted new policies and guidance.

Ideally, any previous approvals should be "live", but even if an approval has expired (i.e. the development was not carried out within three years from when the decision was made), it carries some weight. It there has been no change in the context (the physical setting, the relevant planning policies) the council should not refuse something that was approved several years before.

It is a common strategy to submit a series of applications, slowly chipping away at the council's objections. If, for example, you expect the planners to balk at a proposal for a host of front, side and rear extensions, you don't want to provoke a wholesale refusal. You might start with applying only for part of the development, and securing permission for that before applying for the rest. For example, you might apply for a single-storey rear extension on its own. If that was approved, you might apply for the same extension *and* a side extension. The council, having already approved the rear, should focus on the new elements of the application.

If you are planning to extend your house to the side and convert the extension into a separate dwelling, you might apply in two separate steps. If you apply for both steps at once, and the case officer doesn't like the idea of a new house being created in that location, they may find reason to object to both the extension and the conversion, even though it may only be the conversion that raises concerns. By obtaining permission for the extension first, you reduce the risk of an objection to the physical development being proposed at the site and can focus on obtaining consent for the conversion.

FALLBACK POSITIONS

A **fallback position** is a backup plan – a development that you could carry out if your current proposal is refused permission. Fallback positions are an important material consideration in the assessment of planning applications and can be used to your advantage.

Say, for example, you want planning permission for a five-metre-deep ground floor rear extension to a detached house. You have permitted development rights for a four-metre-deep extension. It is reasonable to assume that if you are not granted permission for the five-metre extension, you will simply build the four-metre extension. The key issue to be assessed, therefore, is whether the additional one-metre depth of your proposal, relative to your fallback position, causes harm in planning terms.

Similarly, imagine you obtain planning permission for a bungalow on land to the side of your existing house. Later, you decide that you would like to have a taller, two-storey house. Your fallback position, if permission is refused, is to build the bungalow as originally planned. The council must take this into account – they cannot argue that it is not an appropriate site for a house of any kind, for example.

Creating or highlighting a fallback position is a common strategy for developments in the green belt. As discussed earlier, government policy limits extensions to houses in the green belt and councils often apply a numerical limit (limiting extensions to a 40 percent increase in the size of the original house, for example). However, most houses in the green belt still have permitted development rights. If you are applying for an extension that exceeds the council's limits but an alternative permitted development extension (i.e. something you don't need permission for at all) would arguably cause even greater harm to the openness of the green belt, you could attempt to trade one against the other. If the council is persuaded that you will resort to building an alternative extension under permitted development if planning permission is withheld, they may consider that to be a valid fallback position and grant permission for what you have proposed.

For the fallback argument to work, it needs to be likely that you will implement your backup plan. Applicants sometimes draw up plans for a range of ugly extensions allowed under permitted development and use this to support a planning application for the extensions they really want, which are less ugly. If the council is not persuaded you will truly build out the alternative extensions, the fallback position has no force. It is nevertheless worth keeping in mind that, if your proposal is likely to be controversial, it may be a good tactic to apply for something that you don't really want, but is likely to be approved, as a stepping stone to getting approval for what you do want.

If a case officer does not like a scheme, they tend to pile on reasons for refusal that are unrelated to their concerns. Say, for example, that you think the council will be happy to approve a bungalow on a site but will be less inclined to approve a two-storey house, on the basis that it would be too tall. If you apply for the two-storey house, you might find it refused – not just on the basis that it is too tall, but also because there isn't enough parking, for example (as the case officer tries to strengthen the refusal by finding other concerns). Had you first applied for the bungalow – and had it approved – you would have resolved the parking issue prior to the resubmission for the two-storey proposal.

Don't Be Misled by "Precedent"

Most of the clients who approach us for help with tricky planning problems do not have a good idea of exactly how the planning system works but instinctively feel that the council's decision is wrong. This is often because they have seen examples around their area of the type of extension they want and they don't see why they shouldn't be allowed to build the same thing. They believe that a **precedent** has been set.

Every area has its eye-catching developments, not all of them sensitive additions to the streetscape. Though neighbouring developments can be a guide to what is possible, one must exercise caution. You do not have the right to build something simply because some of your neighbours have. Certainly, the council has some explaining to do if it grants one neighbour permission for an extension but refuses another for more or less the same thing. There is an expectation that council decision-making is consistent – that it is a matter of fairness.

But applications are assessed in line with policies and other material considerations. If a proposal represents unacceptably bad design or it is expected that it will harm a neighbour's living conditions, it should be refused consent even if the council granted someone else in the area permission for something similar. The council regrets some of its decisions and resolves not to make the same mistake twice.

Some clients send us through photographs of other extensions in the area that are "even uglier than mine" (though they may not put it quite like that). It offends their sense of fairness that someone else has been able to build a monstrosity, but they cannot. However, an application is doomed to failure if your argument is that your ugly development is not as bad as some of the other eyesores in the area. Two wrongs do not make a right. In this respect, the importance of precedent in planning is misunderstood. There is a mistaken impression that planners decide applications by looking around the immediate area to see if other people have done the same thing. That is not how it works.

The truth is that, in any area, all sorts of extensions have been built. Some were built many moons ago, when planning policies and permitted development rules were different. Councils generally hate front dormer roof extensions, for example. The reason that some areas have so many of them is because they were once permitted development (but aren't any longer). Some were built without planning permission or built larger than their planning permission (or permitted development rights) allowed. Some were granted permission, but perhaps shouldn't have been. Some are subject to enforcement action and may one day need to be demolished.

The fact that other houses on your street have front dormers clearly helps your case but does not guarantee a positive outcome. It helps if the number of dormers means that the character of the area has changed sufficiently so that your proposal will fit in well and not look out of place. If the existing dormers are ugly and yours will exacerbate the harm, your proposal will not be successful.

THE MOST POPULAR HOUSEHOLDER DEVELOPMENTS

In this section, I look at the most common householder developments and how they are assessed. Remember that this is a guide only – the approach taken by each council differs greatly, so always look at specific local policies and guidance. Remember that you may not need planning permission at all for the developments below. They may be permitted development (i.e. development for which express planning permission is not required) – revisit Step 2 for more on this.

Single-Storey Rear Extensions

Ground floor rear extensions are undoubtedly the most common form of householder development – a relatively quick, cheap, and easy way to extend your downstairs reception space, usually to create a roomy, open-plan kitchen/diner.

Under permitted development, you can (usually) extend directly to the rear, to a depth of three metres (on a terraced or semi-detached house) or four metres (on a detached house). These limits are doubled under the larger home extensions scheme and subject to neighbour consent. The extension can be up to three metres high to the eaves and four metres to the top of the roof.

As I explained in Step 2, not all houses (and no flats) have permitted development rights and planning permission is required for all extensions. Most councils have guidance that borrows from the PD criteria to similarly limit extensions to three or four metres, where a property cannot take advantage of permitted development rights and full planning permission is required. They may also limit the height of the extension. You can extend to a greater depth if you can show that "other material considerations" justify it. As the extension is to the rear and probably low in height, there is not usually a concern about its design and appearance. The primary issue is whether it harms neighbours' living conditions. Whether it does or not is a function of its proximity to the boundary and to the neighbour, its height, its depth, and the relative orientation of the properties.

You may consider ways in which you can design your extension to reduce the impact on your neighbours. A flat roof may have less impact that a pitched or hipped roof. Though most extensions are around three metres high, a development will have less impact if it slopes down to 2.5 metres or even two metres along the neighbour's boundary, as shown in figure 23.

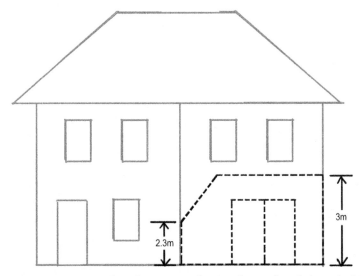

Figure 23: An extension may have less impact if its height is reduced along the boundary

Alternatively, you could set part or all of your extension away from the boundary – stepping it in progressively, perhaps, as it projects deeper into the garden. In figure 24, one extension runs along the boundary with the neighbour to a depth of three metres and is then set two metres away from the boundary; in the other example, the extension is set in one metre from the neighbour's boundary for its full depth.

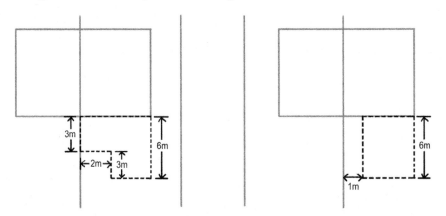

Figure 24: An extension may have less impact if it steps away from the boundary

If there is only one neighbour who might be affected, you should ask them whether they have any plans to extend. A joint application would stand a better chance of success – your extension cannot have an impact on your neighbour if they build a matching structure at the same time. If the council neglects to put a condition on your planning approval, insisting that both extensions are built simultaneously, you might even be able to go ahead with yours even if your neighbour abandons their own plans.

My colleagues and I at Just Planning appeal a huge number of refusals for single-storey rear extensions each year and we have a high success rate. Case officers have difficulty assessing these applications. A ground-floor rear extension to any depth will have some impact on neighbours if the house to be extended is one in a row of tightly-packed terraced houses. It is very difficult to identify the depth at which this impact becomes unacceptably harmful. In the past, a line was drawn in the sand at three or four metres deep, but more generous permitted development rules (allowing extensions of six or eight metres) have set the cat among the pigeons. If one can build to six metres without needing planning permission (and subject to prior approval – see Step 2), what justification is there for refusing planning permission for the same development? When in doubt, case officers tend to refuse permission. The householder planning system as a whole is moving towards much greater flexibility for single-storey rear extensions and this is reflected in our success rate at appeal.

FIRST-FLOOR REAR EXTENSIONS

Single-storey rear extensions are common and fairly straightforward. First-floor rear extensions are much more difficult. In a nutshell, their elevated position causes more harm to neighbours. A taller, two-storey structure close to the neighbour's boundary is much more likely to cause overshadowing and to have an overbearing or oppressive visual impact.

It is for this reason that PD rights only allow two-storey rear extensions where the development as a whole is set away at least two metres from the boundaries. As this is difficult to achieve on smaller plots, first-floor rear extensions generally require planning permission. When applying for planning permission, it is best to curb your ambitions. The shallower and narrower your extension, the more likely it is to find favour.

Lots of councils apply the 45-degree rule when assessing first floor rear extensions. It is considered likely that an extension will lead to a loss of light affecting a neighbour's window if the extension breaches an imaginary line drawn at 45 degrees from the middle of that window, as shown in figure 25. So, if you share a party wall with a neighbour (if your house is terraced or semi-detached), it is likely that you will have to set your extension away from the boundary to avoid the 45-degree line.

Single-storey extensions are low in height and are not prominent when viewed from neighbouring houses. First-floor extensions can have a much greater visual impact. As a rule of thumb, they should not project to a depth of more than 2.5 or three metres. They are unlikely, otherwise, to be subordinate to the host property.

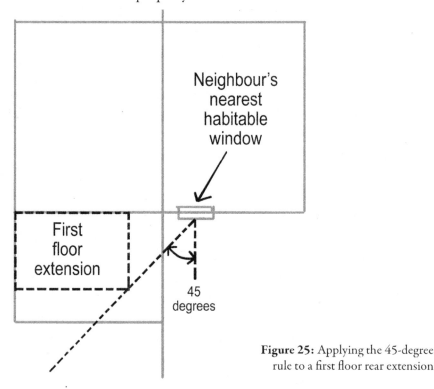

Figure 25: Applying the 45-degree rule to a first floor rear extension

Two-Storey Side Extensions

Planners are cautious about side extensions because they are visible from the street. Single-storey side extensions are permitted development (as long as they are no wider than 50 percent of the width of the original house), but first-floor side extensions need planning permission.

There are, broadly, two design approaches for two-storey side extensions: for them to appear as subordinate additions set back from the original house, or for them to appear as a continuation of the existing building.

For semi-detached houses with an asymmetric design and a distinctive architectural composition (bay windows, hipped roofs, etc) setting the extension back is usually best – the new extension is clearly distinct from, and subordinate to, the main house. For a terraced house with a plain front elevation, a continuation of the front wall, so that the old and the new blend seamlessly, may be a superior approach.

As always, defer to a competent designer. But also be aware of any local planning policies and guidance. Councils commonly insist that side extensions are set back one metre from the front elevation of the existing house, as shown in figure 26. It is best to comply with this unless an exception is justified. A setback may not be necessary where your extension will integrate comfortably with the design and proportions of the main house, or where your proposed extension matches a number of others in the immediate area. Remember that council case officers cling stubbornly to their adopted guidance, so be prepared to appeal if the decision does not go your way.

Planners are also concerned about the possibility of what they call the **terracing effect**. This is where two semi-detached houses both extend to the side, on to the boundary, so that the gap between them is removed. The result is the creation of what appears to be a terraced row, as shown in figure 27. Case officers sometimes object to this where it occurs, but the important thing is not whether a terracing effect is created but whether that effect causes unacceptable harm to the streetscene. Where large numbers of houses on the street have extended in the same way, and the terracing effect is part of its new, established character, planning permission should be granted.

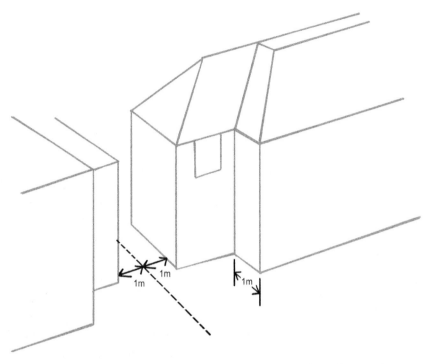

Figure 26: For two-storey side extensions, councils often request setbacks from the front and side

Avoid excessively wide side extensions. Some properties are blessed with unusually wide side gardens. If the width of a side extension is around 50 percent of the width of the main house, the extension will not dominate the building and is more likely to appear as a complementary addition. A side extension that doubles the width of the house is much more likely to appear out of place. To get an extension of this size through, you will need to shell out more for a thoughtful design. If your side garden is unusually large, you should also consider whether you should indeed be applying for planning permission for a whole new dwelling in your side garden.

Finally, planners are wary of side extensions to corner houses. Gaps to the sides of corner houses were designed into housing estates by their architects to create some openness. Houses built right up to the boundaries, or corners, can be oppressive. Some councils ask that extensions are set one metre away, for example, from the boundary with the street, others that they don't stick out beyond the front elevations of the houses on the street behind (known as the "reverse building line"). As ever, this is about good design and about reading the existing character of the area. How distinctive are the corner gaps and what contribution do they make to the quality of the surrounding streetscape? If the answer is little, and if other houses or comparable corners have been extended, you have a good chance of getting permission.

Figure 27: The terracing effect

Roof Level Extensions

Loft conversions with dormer roof extensions are the best way to add bedrooms to your home. Ground floor extensions mainly add reception space and first floor rear and side extensions are tricky to get permission for and add relatively little floor area. A converted loft, with large rear dormer, can add up to two bedrooms and a bathroom.

The problem is that there is a stark contrast between what you can build under permitted development and what you will be granted planning permission for. I take dozens of cases every year where a householder has built a dormer under PD, fallen into one of the traps discussed in Step 2 and is faced with having to demolish the whole thing.

Almost all councils resist the full-sized rear dormers that are commonplace in urban areas in England. Where planning permission is required (because the building is converted into flats, its PD rights were removed by condition, or it is in a conversation area, for example) the dormer will be limited to around half the size of a full-sized, PD extension.

The detailed guidance varies from council to council. Some will advise that dormers be set away from the sides of the roof or that they do not "dominate" the roof. Others have specific limits – that a dormer is set back one metre from the eaves, down 0.5 metres from the ridge and away 0.5 metres from each of the sides, for example. A dormer with these dimensions is sometimes of little use – if the dormer is set away from the side walls, it will not provide enough head height for a staircase to be built up from the floor below (unless the staircase is created right in the middle of the first-floor bedrooms). In many cases, this guidance makes a loft conversion impractical.

As large box dormers have spread like a rash across our towns and cities, case officers and appeal inspectors have been showing some flexibility. If close neighbours have large box dormers, it is highly likely that you will be granted permission for one. If not, you should certainly consider an appeal.

OUTBUILDINGS

The permitted development rights for outbuildings are generous so, like dormer loft extensions, most people take advantage of them where they can. If you need full planning permission, you may run into planners' paranoia that you intend to create "beds in sheds" – building a garden structure to rent out as separate living accommodation (on Airbnb, perhaps).

Outbuildings should be "domestic" in size and scale and not compete with the main house, which should remain the dominant structure on the site. The planners will usually expect to see them at the side and back and they should be single-storey and low in height. Provide a detailed explanation of what you need the space for – submit a detailed layout on the floorplans for example – to assuage any concerns about your true intentions. As with all forms of development, you will have a better chance of success if neighbours have built similar and yours will therefore fit in neatly with the surrounding area.

It can be difficult to obtain permission for granny annexes. The planners are concerned that they will ultimately be rented out as separate dwellings (granny will pass away eventually), and they don't like to see entire new dwellings built at the end of someone's garden. It is easier to obtain consent if the accommodation is not fully self-contained; if it does not have a kitchen, for example, and granny uses the main house for her meals. Some councils will allow fully self-contained granny annexes but will attach a condition requiring that they be used only by members of the main house and not as a separate, self-contained dwellings. Under those circumstances, if an annexe was later let out, the council could take enforcement action against a breach of condition. It is a good idea, before you apply, to find out how your own council approaches this form of development. Take some advice from a local planning consultant or check out the council's planning website to see how similar applications have been treated in recent months.

PORCHES

Most of my clients think of porches and front boundaries (i.e. front walls, gates or fences along the street) as minor developments and uncontroversial. However, these forms of development can really irritate the planners. A badly designed porch can harm the character of a house and, if the house is one of a uniform row of similar dwellings, harm the streetscene as well. Porches are often permitted development – if two metres away from the boundary with the highway, no more than three metres tall and with a floor area of no more than three square metres. If your porch is not PD, take special care to ensure it is carefully designed and complements your property.

Front Boundaries

Planners like low, unobtrusive front boundaries – a low brick wall or a one-metre-high fence. Homeowners like tall, imposing boundaries – it makes them feel safer. Some build two-metre-high railings or fences, assuming that the council will not possibly object. Sadly, they often do, and we have a low success rate at appeal when it comes to tall front boundaries. Unless most of your neighbours have taller boundaries, it is best to stick with the one metre that you are allowed under permitted development.

Mega Extensions

In the sections above, I have provided some advice on how various types of householder extensions are assessed by local planners. However, much of my consultancy work relates to what might be called "mega extensions". High rates of stamp duty incentivise families to extend rather than move and it is possible to combine all of the extensions above, doubling the floor area of your house with side and rear extensions, and a loft conversion. Figure 28 shows a combination of rear extensions at ground, first and second floor levels.

This must be handled carefully – planners are reluctant to approve more comprehensive schemes. The easiest approach is to submit a single application for the entire development. If it is well designed, complies with the council's policies and guidance, fits in with a varied streetscene, and doesn't harm the neighbours, it should be approved. If you expect to face resistance, then you may prefer to take an incremental approach. It is best to seek the help of a planning consultant in devising a strategy, but a mix of permitted development and planning applications may achieve the desired result. It is common, for example, to submit applications for certificates of lawfulness to establish what elements are permitted development and then reapply, seeking planning permission for a combination of the permitted development extensions and the additional elements that require full planning permission. This kind of approach can take a year or more but may be worth it if it ultimately gets you the extensions you want.

Be careful not to stumble into enforcement problems. If you obtain prior approval for a six-metre-deep ground floor extension under permitted development, for example, that consent is only valid as long as the extension is built in isolation. It cannot be combined with a first-floor rear extension approved through a planning application (unless that planning application also showed the ground floor element, of course, or unless you build the ground floor and only then apply for the first-floor addition afterwards). As ever, seek professional advice.

Figure 28: A "mega extension" (combined ground, first and second floor extensions)

Step 3 Summary

1. Planners have quite a lot of discretion and some of their decisions are questionable, to say the least. But there is some predictability in the system.
2. Decisions should be made in accordance with planning policies. It is a good idea to become familiar with the policies (and supplementary guidance) relevant to your area and development.
3. But planning policies are not the end of the story. There are other material considerations – the character of the area, the relationship of your property to its neighbours, the planning history, any fallback positions and more.
4. To get a good sense of how policies and considerations are applied, look up similar applications on the council's website. Read the officer's report for a unique insight into how the planners assess other applications.
5. If in doubt, call the duty planning officer at your local council (the planner on duty on any given day to respond to residents' queries).
6. Planners are supposed to weigh up all of the competing considerations in the planning balance. The next chapter helps you manage the case officer and the application process to load the scales in your favour.

Step 4:
Apply Tactically and Effectively

Congratulations on getting this far! You have already done most of the hard work: you have found a good designer, worked out what you really need, determined that you need to apply for planning permission, and familiarised yourself with local policies. Now it's time to turn all that hard work into an actual planning application and do what you can to get it approved.

What's the secret? You must submit complete and accurate information, manage case officers with care, view pre-application advice with caution, communicate with your neighbours and councillors, and try to pre-empt planning conditions.

THE NUTS AND BOLTS OF MAKING AN APPLICATION

Applications are submitted online through the government's **planning portal** (planningportal.co.uk) and forwarded to your local council. In most cases, your agent will make the application for you, so a detailed run-through of how to complete the application is outside the scope of this book. It is not particularly complicated but can be bureaucratic and much easier for those who have done it before.

However, it is not a good idea to sit back and let your agent take all the strain. Many designers love the process of meeting the client, understanding the site, and creating a beautiful set of plans, but they hate the messiness of dealing with the planning application process itself. Some simply submit and then move onto their next project. Therefore, it is important for you to be clear on how your agent intends to manage the application and when you should expect updates.

The first step on the journey is validation, in which the council makes sure that the application is complete, has no obvious mistakes and that the correct fee has been paid. This is where the anguish usually starts.

THE EXTRAORDINARY FRUSTRATIONS OF VALIDATION

Validation should be a straightforward process, but it can be the most frustrating part of the whole journey. Validation officers are often the most junior members of the team, and not usually planners. It can be difficult for them to understand the nature of the applications before them and exercise judgement in what plans and documents to request.

Some councils have painfully slow validation teams – in one council I worked for, applications were sometimes validated six weeks after receipt and just a couple of weeks before the eight-week deadline for a final decision. This was frustrating for applicants and their agents and made life difficult for case officers.

Others invalidate applications in order to restart the clock and to buy more time for decision-making. This is actually a consequence of the strict eight-week target for deciding applications. By telling the applicant that the application is invalid (due to some minor error on the plans or application form) the council has more time to process it. It is infuriating to submit an application and discover several weeks later that the council has not yet started the clock.

Some of the issues are petty: demands for additional plans or arguments over very minor drafting errors or requests for bat surveys to be carried out in buildings very unlikely to house bats, for example. Unreasonable demands would not necessarily be a problem if it was possible to have a reasonable conversation with the officer about how to meet them. But, like planning officers, validation officers can have tin ears. It is increasingly rare for them to provide a telephone number with which to contact them, and if you email back your protests, they may take a further two weeks before replying, in effect, that "computer says no". As a result, the only option is to comply with their requests, even if it wastes time and involves unnecessary expense.

CASE STUDY: A REAR EXTENSION MIRED IN RED TAPE

I recently applied on behalf of a client in a London borough for rear extensions to his house. Before validating the application, the council requested the preparation and submission of a Demolition and Construction Management and Logistics Plan to include detailed information on:

1. *details of the routing of construction vehicles to the site, hours of access, access and egress arrangements within the site, and security procedures;*

2. *site preparation and construction stages of the development;*

3. *details of provisions for recycling of materials, the provision on site of a storage/delivery area for all plant, site huts, site facilities, and materials;*

123

4. *details showing how all vehicles associated with the construction works would be properly washed and cleaned to prevent the passage of mud and dirt onto the adjoining highway;*

5. *the methods to be used and the measures to be undertaken to control the emission of dust, noise, and vibration arising from construction works;*

6. *a suitable and efficient means of suppressing dust, including the adequate containment of stored or accumulated material so as to prevent it becoming airborne at any time and giving rise to nuisance;*

7. *noise mitigation measures for all plant and processors;*

8. *details of contractors' compound and car parking arrangements;*

9. *details of interim car parking management arrangements for the duration of construction;*

10. *details of a community liaison contact for the duration of all works associated with the development;*

11. *details of measures to mitigate impacts on pedestrian and cyclist movements in proximity to the site;*

12. *details showing that the function and operation of the adjacent bus stop would not be impacted.*

The requirements were obviously grossly disproportionate to the scale of development proposed. The special measures they were requesting were not necessary – they are usually intended for much larger housing developments. The validation officer, who was polite, respectful and well-meaning, would not accept this argument so, in the end, I prepared the report, as requested.

If you consider the council's unwillingness to validate to be unreasonable, you have the right to appeal but this is unrealistic for almost all applicants and I have never recommended that a client appeal a failure to validate – it would take much longer than simply complying with unreasonable requests.

In defence of validation officers, a high proportion of applications are submitted with fundamental errors. Sometimes designers show a window on the elevations but leave it off the floorplans. Or put the wrong scale on the drawing or use the wrong application form. Redbridge Council has become so frustrated with avoidable errors on applications that it now fines the worst offenders a sum of £60. Although anyone can make a mistake, these sins are generally committed by the kind of slapdash designers I warned you about in Step 1. Having followed my advice and chosen a respected local agent, your submission should be free of these kinds of errors.

SUBMITTING COMPLETE APPLICATIONS

Although it costs more upfront, it is a good idea to make your application as complete and detailed as possible. If you are proposing a side extension that will take up some of your driveway, show how you will alter the paving and where the car will be parked. If you plan to hide the bins away in a timber enclosure, provide a drawing showing the precise design and dimensions of this enclosure. As well as avoiding unnecessary conditions, this approach conveys to the case officer that you have properly thought about your application and it is therefore more likely to find favour.

HOW TO MANAGE YOUR CASE OFFICER

Once your application passes validation, it lands on the desk of the case officer. The best case officers have a look through the file to ensure it is error-free and complete, and to check if there is anything they need to do early in the process (such as consult a specialist on some aspect of the proposal). Lots of case officers just add the file to a tottering pile under their desk and return to the applications that are running hard up against their decision deadline.

The government sets targets for public services in order to deliver results. Householder planning applications should be decided within eight weeks. The statutory eight-week target is like the four-hour waiting target in hospital A&E departments – it focuses the minds of public servants but creates all kinds of distortions. Most planning applications are decided in the last few days leading up to the deadline. Almost none are decided before week six of eight. Though case officers are supposed to work with applicants to improve schemes that are not acceptable, there is often no time to seek amendments to the plans. This can mean that a generally good scheme, which might easily have been amended to make it acceptable to the planners, is refused.

The case officer is the single most important person in the planning process. Although they are bound to make decisions consistently and in line with policies and guidance, and can be overruled by senior officers if they reach the wrong conclusion, case officers have wide discretion to reach whatever decision they like. Power corrupts, and not all decisions are fair. Some are unfair because the case officer makes a mistake, some case officers are just not very good at what they do, and many are overworked. Case officers can also be extraordinarily petty. They take against some applicants or their agents or are overly sympathetic to a hysterical objecting neighbour. It is therefore a good idea to get them on your side, and the best opportunity to do this is on the **site visit**.

Make Use of the Site Visit

Planners like to hide behind their desks. Anxious applicants, pushy agents, and aggressive neighbours are difficult to deal with. Planners don't want to get dragged into neighbour disputes. It is easiest to withdraw and make decisions remotely, avoiding direct human contact wherever possible. For most applications, though, they must venture out from the town hall and see the site. This is because, as I explained in Step 3, although they will know what policies and guidance they need to take into account when looking at your plans, there are other material considerations that could sway the decision.

The site visit may be your only chance to speak to the case officer face-to-face. It is much easier for the officer to casually refuse permission for a proposal when the applicant is anonymous. They feel more of an urge to help someone they have met and with whom there is some kind of rapport. Invite them in, offer some tea and tell them why you need the extension, and how it was designed. Point out similar extensions on neighbouring houses and explain why you think yours fits in with the house and the streetscene, and why you don't expect there to be any harm to your neighbours.

There is no need for a heavy sales pitch. Don't overprepare, and don't be pushy. Case officers deal with hundreds of similar applications each year, and they know what is usually allowed and what they can't accept. You probably aren't going to persuade them to grant approval for something they don't think is appropriate. The purpose of the site visit is not to pitch your proposal, but to build a relationship so that the case officer will take your calls, be helpful, and provide some advice if the application is refused.

Do not be afraid to ask the case officer what they think about your proposal. They may choose to be evasive but also could provide some useful advice. If you are heading for a refusal, it is good to know early on in the process. If you need to revise your plans (usually by making the extension smaller), you have a rare opportunity here to get a clear idea from the case officer on what they would recommend.

Neighbour Objections Are Important, but Not Usually Decisive

Councils have a legal obligation to consult neighbours on planning applications, and to give them at least 21 days in which to respond. If neighbours write to object after the 21-day consultation period has ended, but before the decision has been made, their representations must still be taken into account.

Neighbours may be consulted by letter or the application may be advertised in a local newspaper or by way of a notification attached to lampposts close to the property. It is up to the council to decide who must be consulted and the officers do not always get it right. In a recent application for a new floor to be added to a 15-storey block of flats, Hackney Council consulted all of the flats in neighbouring blocks but none of the 45 flats in the block itself (I represented the flat owners objecting to the proposal).

The council will also consult the local parish or town council, if there is one. If you revise your plans during the application process, neighbours will usually be re-consulted (often to their confusion). Anyone can object to an application, even if they live many miles away and have no obvious interest in the site. Some people amuse themselves by objecting to random applications across their local area – each council has one or two local residents who take an interest in virtually all applications the planners receive.

Case officers do not really pay close attention to neighbours' objections. They deal with hundreds of householder applications a year and have a pretty good idea of what they will approve or refuse. Whether an extension is of poor design or harms neighbouring properties is a matter separate from whether neighbours *think* an extension is badly designed or affects their living conditions.

If the council's position is that extensions deeper than three metres will overshadow neighbours, they will refuse permission even if the affected neighbour writes in support of the proposal. They will not be more inclined to refuse if the neighbour writes to object to the scheme.

Neighbours rarely make very effective representations. Many raise issues that are not material planning considerations – concerns about drainage, or a boundary dispute or the impact on the value of their property. They complain about a loss of light when the proposed extension is set several metres away. They cast aspersions about the applicant's character or complain about his inconsiderate late-night parties – these are not planning considerations. In many cases, neighbour objections are aggressive, shrill, unfocused, and unreasonable. Case officers scan their contents for key words and then file them away.

Homeowners who contact us for advice have an exaggerated sense of the importance of the neighbours' opinions. They rage that the planners refused permission even though the neighbour had no objection. They assume that if a neighbour objected and the application was later refused, the neighbour must have exerted some undue influence on the planning officers. The reality is that neighbours do not have a strong sense of whether an extension is appropriate in planning terms. It is difficult for them to judge if their living conditions will be harmed. And they are not dispassionate observers.

It is also worth bearing in mind that extensions are forever. They are permanent structures that may long outlive current residents. It is the impact on *notional* current and future residents of the house that is important, even if the actual residents have no real objection to what is proposed. The case officer's role is largely to establish objectively whether a development harms living conditions. It is not fair to expect neighbours to make that judgement.

There are some cases in which neighbour objections can make a difference, sometimes inadvertently. Say, for example, an extension is proposed next to a small side window on the neighbour's house and the case officer decides that it is probably a window to a non-habitable room (a utility room or a hallway, say) and therefore doesn't benefit from special protection. If the neighbour objects and points out that this is, in fact, the only window to a downstairs bedroom, that changes the case officer's assessment. The council may accept a loss of light to a utility room or hallway, where residents do not spend much time, but would be concerned about the same loss of light to a bedroom.

The reverse is also true: neighbours sometimes write in to complain about the likely impact of an extension on their utility room window, thereby sealing their fate by letting the case officer know that the window in question does not serve a habitable room.

Neighbours can also highlight material planning concerns that an officer has missed, for instance that land levels are lower on their side of the fence, meaning a proposed extension will appear taller from the neighbour's garden.

In some cases, the trigger for an application to be taken away from a case officer and decided by councillors on the planning committee is a certain number of neighbour objections. Planning decisions made by councillors on the committee are much more questionable than those made by professional planners, and it is usually better if your application does not get called in to committee.

Some residents start petitions or photocopy and distribute standardised objection letters for neighbours to send in. Petitions and copy-and-paste objection letters do not carry any weight and are a waste of time. Angry, orchestrated campaigns can backfire if they are too aggressive, by generating sympathy for the applicant.

Having said that, a large number of angry objection letters is usually a sign of public concern, even to a tin-eared case officer. One or two objections might be brushed off, but several warrant a little more investigation. Case officers, and councils in general, are more cautious about granting permission in the face of vocal opposition – they like an easy life, after all. If a proposal is acceptable in planning terms, but has generated opposition, some councils will decide that it is better to refuse, assuming the applicant will just appeal the decision and get permission that way (this "planning by appeal" approach to decision-making is discussed further in the next chapter).

This is more of a problem with larger, more controversial applications than with applications for humble householder extensions. However, if you are concerned about the possibility of neighbour objections derailing your plans, it is best to take a copy round to them (perhaps with a peace-making bottle of wine) before you submit your application, in an effort to gain their support before the consultation letters land on their doormats.

Also remember that, if planning permission is granted, you will of course need to build the extension, and an angry neighbour could make that process more difficult. Neighbours who feel that they have not been kept informed or treated fairly can become difficult during the construction process. If they complain to the council about the building work, you could receive unwelcome visits from the planning enforcement team. Best to keep neighbours onside, where possible.

CASE STUDY: SAVE THE BOOKSHOP!

In 2019, I represented the owner of a shop in Cornwall who had been renting it to a second-hand bookseller for more than 20 years. My client wanted to retire and fund his retirement by developing and selling the premises. I advised him that the shop was worth more as a two-bedroom flat and that he could take advantage of permitted development rights (Schedule 2, Part 3, Class M: Conversion of Retail to Residential) to convert the shop into a flat without having to apply for full planning permission.

Though full planning permission was not required, it was still necessary to apply for prior approval – a form of light-touch application to check that the proposal would meet the permitted development criteria. The application generated intense local opposition – there were 276 objections from local residents, revealing the depth of affection that the community had for the bookshop.

However, the planning system does not (usually) protect a particular occupier – the council can apply policies protecting retail uses in general, but not a much-loved local bookshop in particular. Despite the intensity of local opposition, the application was approved. The bookshop is now a flat and, happily, the bookseller found new premises nearby and is still in business.

THE "PRE-APP" TRAP

When councils refuse planning permission, they often add a note to the end of the decision notice stating out that the applicant did not seek **pre-application advice** before submitting their application. It implies, a little cattily, that if their advice had been sought, the unpleasantness of a planning refusal could have been avoided.

Planning departments will provide very general advice on demand and for free (through their duty planning service), but if you want advice on a specific site or proposal, they will direct you to their pre-application service. The hope is that, through engaging with the council relatively early in the design process, any issues will be ironed out and a much better application will be submitted, with a much-improved chance of success.

Councils have been promoting their pre-application services more energetically in recent years because they can now charge for them and as such they are a valued source of income (planning application fees are otherwise set nationally and only cover an estimated 50 percent of the cost of running a planning department). Not all councils charge, though, and pre-application advice for householder development (extensions, etc.) is sometimes still free.

Though the conventional wisdom is that seeking pre-application advice is a good idea, it can sometimes be a trap. A good designer will be familiar with the council's policies and guidance and will have a general idea of how the application will be considered. That part of the pre-application response should not be particularly enlightening. Lots of proposals, though, have some aspects that are finely balanced – they may not fully comply with adopted policies but can still be justified. The rationale for seeking pre-application advice is that you obtain the informal opinion of a case officer in advance of an application, to avoid an unnecessary refusal.

The disadvantages are myriad, though. Firstly, it takes time. Ninety percent of minor planning applications are determined in eight weeks. There is no statutory timeframe for pre-application advice. The last time I submitted a pre-application on a project, I waited four months for a response. By going ahead and submitting a planning application instead, I would have saved half that time. When it came to deciding the subsequent planning application, the advice set out by the case officer in the pre-application response was overruled by a more senior officer, who took an entirely different position.

Secondly, it can be expensive. Though most councils do not charge householders, a lot of the London boroughs do. Camden charges £433 for pre-application advice on an extension but a planning application for the same development is just £206. If you want to know whether your extension might be granted permission in Camden, it would be both quicker and cheaper to apply for permission directly.

Thirdly, you do not always get a clear or useful response. A formal planning application forces a council to come to a final and formal decision. It must weigh up the planning merits, compromise where appropriate, and decide whether or not to grant consent. If refusing the application, the council must set out what aspects of the proposal *were* acceptable and narrow down their concerns to specific reasons for refusal.

In a pre-application response, the case officer has the opportunity to sit on the fence. There is no obligation to make a firm decision on a finely-balanced issue. It is common to receive a response that lays out both sides of the argument but does not settle the question. The pre-app does not, in any case, bind the council to a future decision on a planning application; it is common to receive an encouraging response at pre-application stage, but be refused planning permission when the application is submitted, because a more senior officer takes a different position to the case officer who provided the initial advice.

The greatest disadvantage is that pre-apps give the council an opportunity to set out a shopping list of requirements. There is no such thing as a "perfect" application and the pre-application process can give the council the opportunity to comment on negative aspects of a proposal that might be tolerated, on balance, when weighed up as part of a complete planning application. In situations where you have a considered and relatively uncomplicated proposal, entering into the pre-application process can open a can of worms.

It is worth seeking pre-application advice, however, for complicated proposals where you really need a steer from a case officer or where the application is sensitive and you would like a discussion with the officer before it is made public through the formal application process. The other advantage of the pre-application process is that it gives you the opportunity to meet the case officer, establish a one-to-one rapport, and "pitch" your proposal (as much as it is possible to do so).

THE BURDEN OF EXPENSIVE REPORTS

It is right that the planning system should seek to control, avoid or mitigate the harmful impacts of development. The burden falls on the applicant to show that their proposals will not cause unacceptable harm. Where councils suspect harm may be caused, they have the power to ask applicants to demonstrate that it will not.

Increasingly, councils take a precautionary approach, asking for detailed surveys and reports to be submitted where a development might have harmful impacts. Case officers are not really sympathetic to the burden this places on applicants who are proposing small-scale developments. They can also be reluctant to exercise their discretion to release these applicants from the obligation to commission expensive survey reports in cases where they are not strictly necessary.

If you have sought pre-application advice, you should have a list of what reports the council expects to see (though, as explained above, you cannot always rely on the accuracy or helpfulness of pre-app responses). Otherwise, you should refer to the council's **local list**, a formally adopted document that sets out what is required to make an application valid. Councils are required to publish the local list on their websites, but they are not always up to date and not, therefore, as useful as they could be.

If there are trees on the site, especially trees protected by a Tree Preservation Order (TPO), you will need an **arboricultural report**. If the land may be contaminated (if industrial processes were formerly carried out on it, for example), you will need a contamination assessment. An ecological report will be necessary if your project might affect protected species – bats and owls in buildings that are being converted, newts and other aquatic reptiles, and bats roosting in trees. In **flood zones** you will need a flood risk assessment. If you are providing limited off-street parking, you may need a highways assessment or a parking beat survey (where parking capacity on surrounding streets is measured). Many councils require energy statements setting out how your development will be designed to minimise carbon emissions. If your property is listed or the site is in a conservation area, you may be asked for a heritage statement. Each report costs from £600 to £2,000. The costs quickly mount and can be disproportionate to the scale of small developments.

Oddly, the validation officers insist that the reports are provided, but make no judgement about the contents. I have in the past, and *in extremis*, submitted single-page Microsoft Word documents with the report title at the top ("Energy Statement" for example) and a couple of paragraphs of waffle underneath. The validation officers, happy that a statement had now been submitted, validated the applications and they were later approved without any additional information being requested.

CASE STUDY: A BLIZZARD OF PLANNING REPORTS

I recently submitted an application on behalf of a client in London who wanted an extension to an existing basement flat. The works would involve some excavation into the rear garden, but the floor area of the extension itself was very modest. After the application was submitted, the council responded to request that the following reports be prepared and submitted:

- *Design & Access Statement;*
- *Planning Statement;*
- *Construction Method Statement;*
- *Construction Traffic Management Plan;*
- *Noise, Vibration and Dust Mitigation Measures;*
- *Community Infrastructure Levy (CIL) form;*
- *Tree Report/Survey;*
- *Flood Risk Assessment;*
- *Demonstration of Sustainable Urban Drainage System (SUDS) compliance.*

It was a frustratingly long list of reports for such a small development. Though it is always worth discussing the council's requirements with the case officer and validation officer, it is rare that they will back down, unless you can very clearly show that a particular report is not required. The path of least resistance is usually to supply the information that has been requested.

In this case, I prepared some brief documents myself and worked with specialist consultants on some of the other documents. Most were just a couple of pages long. The process added to the applicant's costs but contributed little in real, tangible planning terms.

INFLUENCING INTERNAL CONSULTEES

Case officers do not have detailed knowledge of the technical aspects of planning applications, such as highways, flood risk, land contamination, and protected trees. They rely on support from internal specialists who are consulted on relevant applications. These specialists receive a copy of the plans and associated documents and are asked to provide a written response.

These consultees are not planners, so they provide information only on their specialist area. They may not have a good knowledge of how to apply planning policies, consider material considerations or assess whether a concern about an application could be resolved by use of a planning condition or by requesting amendments to the plans. It is the role of the case officer to weigh up the various considerations, including consultation responses, and come to a balanced opinion (known as the **planning balance**).

For example, a case officer might decide that, though a highways officer has objected to a proposal that does not quite meet local parking standards, the application should nevertheless be granted permission because it involves the redevelopment of an abandoned site and therefore improves the appearance of the area (the latter consideration outweighing the former).

In practice, however, case officers do not always have the confidence to make these decisions and an objection from a consultee can therefore be fatal to your prospects. Consultees are asked to provide an opinion and may give it quickly without properly assessing the plans and taking all considerations into account. They will not usually visit the site. It is a good idea, therefore, to try and influence the consultee in advance to ensure that they are in full possession of the facts. You can contact tree officers, conservation officers, and the highways team directly for advice. Some have their own (usually free) pre-application services. Many officers are very happy to advise and to assist and they are much less likely to object to an application if they have been involved in its preparation.

ARE PLANNERS CORRUPT?

A surprising number of my clients believe that their application was refused because the planner came under some undue influence. Some assume bribery, others that their neighbour has the ear of a senior council officer.

Brown envelopes are a thing of the past, except in rare cases. Influence may sometimes be brought to bear on big and important planning applications (councils are highly political) but neighbours rarely have that kind of access. In my many years as a case officer, no one ever tried to pay me off (more's the pity) and I have never felt under pressure to make a dodgy decision. I did, however, receive many calls and emails from angry homeowners who had been refused permission, accusing me of accepting a backhander from one of their neighbours.

Councils make some truly awful decisions on householder planning applications. In my experience, and in the vast majority of those cases, the case officer was incompetent rather than corrupt. Either way, you have a remedy – take the decision to appeal (see Step 5).

LOBBYING COUNCILLORS

Councillors are elected to represent their residents. Each ward within a local authority area has its own councillors. If you have submitted a planning application, and have run into difficulty, you can seek help from your local ward councillors.

Council planners may not be sympathetic to the personal circumstances surrounding your application. They assess extensions primarily on their design and the impact on neighbours – the fact that you need a downstairs extension in order to take better care of an elderly relative, for example, may not be given any special weight. A sympathetic councillor could speak to the case officer on your behalf, helping to make your case.

Bear in mind that if your neighbours are concerned about your application, they might also be approaching the councillors and you should ensure that your side of the story is presented – it is not uncommon for councillors to champion the case of the person who gets to them first.

Councillors rarely sway a planning decision, in my experience. They are generally respectful of case officers and the planning process and, though they may call or email an officer for information on an application, they rarely seek to exert any undue pressure. However, case officers take note when an application has generated interest from a councillor and this can, at least, encourage them to look at the application more carefully and closely, perhaps leading to a more considered decision.

THE PLANNING COMMITTEE

Case officers do not decide planning applications, they make *recommendations*. The power to decide a planning application rests with the **planning committee** – a group of elected councillors. However, most applications are decided under **delegated powers**, under which officers can make the decision without deferring to the planning committee.

Each council has a scheme of delegation which determines what applications can be decided by officers and which must come before the committee. It will vary from council to council, but larger applications will always come before the committee and smaller ones will only be considered if a certain number of objections have been received or if a councillor has "called in" the application.

Planning committee meetings are generally held once a month, in the evening, and are open to the public. If your application is to be decided by committee, you (and any objectors) will have the opportunity to address the members. Committee decisions can be erratic. Committee members are not qualified planners and are not necessarily well versed in planning law and practice (how decisions must be made and what counts as a "material consideration") or especially familiar with their own planning policies. They are also subject to pressure from neighbours and local residents, making some decisions more political than technical. Committee members are much more likely than case officers to refuse permission for something they just don't like, even if there are no solid planning grounds for a refusal.

Some applicants like the idea of their application being considered by the planning committee, hoping that the elected members of the committee will approve it even though the case officer intends to issue a refusal. This is usually a forlorn hope. All applications come before committee with a recommendation from the case officer. If an application is called in to committee, and the case officer has recommended refusal, it is rare for the committee to overrule the officer and grant permission. At the end of the day, case officers are the committee's expert advisers and the committee will generally follow their recommendations unless there is good reason to overrule them.

THE WITHDRAWAL METHOD

One of the most common questions our consultants are asked by clients is whether they should withdraw their planning application. This usually follows a conversation with the case officer in which they have said that the proposal is not acceptable and the applicant can avoid a refusal by simply withdrawing the application. This feeds a myth among homeowners that there is something wrong with being refused planning permission. There isn't. If you apply and the council says no, there is nothing to stop you revising and reapplying. You may simply choose to give up and try again in a few years and, although a record of the refusal stays on your file, there is no reason why this should cause you any problems – it doesn't blight the property.

When case officers call to recommend that you withdraw, it is usually just before the end of the eight-week period during which the council is targeted to make their decision. Councils have a "duty to co-operate" and should always work with applicants to amend and improve their applications, where possible. In practice, overworked case officers first look at an application when the eight-week period is about to expire and no longer have time even for the simple amendments that might make an application acceptable.

So why do they suggest withdrawing the application? In most cases, just because writing up their report and preparing a decision notice takes precious time and effort, while a withdrawal is quick and easy. There are also a couple of big advantages to the council in seeing applications withdrawn. The first is that refusal rates are monitored nationwide. In principle, councils with clear policies, good pre-application advice services, and helpful, pro-active case officers should not issue many refusals. More refused applications suggest that councils are not communicating well with their residents.

The second big advantage to the council (and huge disadvantage to you) is that, if the application is voluntarily withdrawn by the applicant, there is no right of appeal. If a planning officer sees minor problems with a scheme (perhaps problems that might be corrected if the eight-week deadline was not looming), there is a risk that a refusal may lead to an appeal, and an embarrassing defeat for the council, including the risk of being required to cover the applicant's appeal costs.

So, should you ever withdraw? Sometimes it is the sensible thing to do. It can be a good way of maintaining a good working relationship with your case officer. Case officers have been known to sweeten their request for a withdrawal by suggesting that your resubmission, with some minor tweaks, will sail through. If the case officer is under pressure with a huge workload and tight deadlines, is willing to work with you to improve your proposal once you resubmit it, and has suggested that it would then be approved, a withdrawal is a worthwhile tactical move.

In most cases, however, you should accept a refusal. This forces the planner to think carefully about exactly what deficiencies the scheme may have, to write a detailed report, and to put together defendable reasons for refusal. If you are very lucky, the case officer was bluffing and the application will be approved. More likely, it is refused but at least you know exactly what the council was concerned about and are well-armed to consider a resubmission or an appeal.

Planning Conditions

If you are granted planning permission (hurrah!), it is likely to be subject to certain conditions (boo!) that are listed on the decision notice. Some conditions are standard to almost all applications. The first is that you have three years in which to start your development. The second condition lists the plans that were submitted and requires that you carry out your development exactly as shown on the plans.

For extensions, the next most common condition is one requiring that the "materials used in the construction of the development match those on the existing house". In other words, if you have a red-brick house with a tiled roof, your extension should be built in red bricks (of a similar shade and texture) and the extension roof should be tiled. This is to ensure that the extension doesn't look out of place as a result of the choice of materials.

If the council has doubts about your ability to choose appropriate materials without direction, it can impose a condition that requires you to submit details of the materials you intend to use so that they can formally approve them before you start work. This kind of condition is known as a **pre-commencement condition** – because it means you cannot commence work until you have obtained approval from the council (until you have "discharged" the condition, in the jargon). Requiring you to submit details is more common in sensitive areas – such as in a conservation area.

Every year I help clients who have built an extension in materials they believe match the main house and have been challenged by the council. It is difficult, of course, to find bricks that match exactly those that were first used to build your house (perhaps hundreds of years ago) and hand-made bricks are much more expensive than the factory-cut, mass-produced equivalents. It is true that a shiny new red brick can look pretty odd next to an old, weathered, non-uniform brick from the eighteenth century.

Most homeowners won't realise their mistake until the extension is built. The good news is that, although the most aggressive councils will consider enforcement action and demand that the extension is torn down, appeals

① council can challenge

inspectors (the individuals who decide planning appeals) tend to take a much more relaxed view of the matter and we have an almost perfect success rate on appeals relating to the choice of materials (see Step 6 for more on householder enforcement issues).

There are usually relatively few additional conditions attached to householder planning approvals. They can include a requirement that:

- no windows are installed in future in the side wall of the new extension (to protect neighbours from overlooking);
- the flat roof on top of a new extension is never used as a roof terrace (also to protect neighbours from overlooking);
- an extension or outbuilding is used only in connection with the main house and is never used as an entirely separate dwelling;
- specified measures are taken to ensure that the building works cause no harm to a nearby protected tree.

Many homeowners and developers pay little attention to the list of conditions attached to the end of their decision notice. They have worked so hard to get permission that they overlook the fact that the consent is conditional. This oversight can be fatal. If you fail to comply with the requirements of a planning condition, you are in **breach of planning control** and at risk of enforcement action for breach of condition. If you start work on a development without first discharging a pre-commencement condition (i.e. you did not first get approval for the materials you have chosen, for example), you have not lawfully commenced your development. After three years, your planning permission will expire. Though you may have carried out your development in that time, because you didn't discharge the pre-commencement conditions the structure may be considered unlawful and you are again at risk of enforcement action.

For this reason, if you are selling or re-mortgaging your home, a solicitor will ask to see a copy of your decision notice to confirm that your extension has planning permission, but should also seek confirmation that the terms of all conditions have been met. As a side note, some conveyancing solicitors don't fully understand the importance of planning conditions – if you are buying a property, ensure that your solicitor does check that the seller has complied with any conditions on planning consents.

CASE STUDY: THE WRONG SHADE OF RED

In 2017, Mr Kumar obtained planning permission for a single-storey side and rear extension to his end-terraced house on the outskirts of Leeds. The decision notice had a standard condition requiring that he use "matching materials". His house was built in red brick with a rendered (and pebble-dashed) front elevation, so he constructed the extension in red brick.

The council served an enforcement notice, arguing that the shade of red he had chosen was much brighter than the bricks on the existing house and that the extension therefore looked out of place. The enforcement notice demanded that the bricks be replaced, which he could not do without demolishing and rebuilding the extension.

I appealed the enforcement notice on Mr Kumar's behalf, pointing out that it is difficult to match new bricks to older bricks that are no longer in production and have, in any case, faded over time. I pointed out that the front elevation of the house was pebble-dashed, so the contrast with the original bricks was not apparent from the street (it was only really noticeable from the rear garden) and that Mr Kumar's bright new bricks matched the facing bricks on a new house that had been built next door, so his extension fitted in well with the streetscene in general. Mr Kumar was delighted when the inspector backed his choice of brick and granted permission for the extension as built.

AVOIDING CONDITIONS

Case officers can be trigger happy when it comes to conditions. They are fearful of missing something out, so load a refusal with anything they might deem necessary. Some conditions are not reasonable and pre-commencement conditions (where you are required to submit specified information to the council before you start work), in particular, will cost you the time and effort of a new application to get them discharged. It is good practice to work with the case officer to minimise the number of conditions. You can avoid a condition requiring approval of materials samples, for example, by sending in the samples with your planning application in the first place.

The government's guidance to councils was always that case officers should engage with applicants to minimise the number of conditions, and to seek their agreement to any pre-commencement conditions before a decision is issued. In 2018, it gave this advice legal grounding through the Town and Country Planning (Pre-commencement Conditions) Regulations, which state that planning permission may not be granted subject to a pre-commencement condition without the written agreement of the applicant to the terms of the condition. The problem is that, when case officers email applicants to request permission to impose a condition, applicants acquiesce rather than risk their application being refused.

If you are granted permission subject to a condition to which you object, you can appeal against the imposition of the planning condition (see the next chapter for more on appeals). The difficulty with this approach is that the appeals inspector, who will decide your appeal, has the power to revisit the whole application and could, in theory, withdraw your approval of planning permission altogether. Rather than appealing against a condition, it is safer to submit a planning application for the **removal or variation of a condition**. If the council refuses to remove or alter the condition, you can then appeal that refusal (and your original planning consent is not at risk).

CONDITIONS REMOVING PERMITTED DEVELOPMENT RIGHTS

When granting permission for new dwellings, councils generally impose a condition removing permitted development rights. This is to stop you building the new house and later taking advantage of PD rights to extend it further than was envisaged in the planning application. This is generally unfair. The purpose of PD rights is to give homeowners permission, in advance, for minor and uncontroversial extensions. The idea is that these rights are granted to almost all houses in the country – they should not be withheld from new houses unless there is a clear justification.

In addition, planning decisions are intended to outlive current occupants. In the case of a brand-new house, future owners of that property may want to extend it for their own reasons and needs. It is unfair that they should not be able to without a full planning application.

The government's planning guidance says that this kind of condition should only be imposed where there is a clear justification. If you are building a new house on a very small site, very close to neighbours, it may be appropriate that more control is exercised over how you extend in future. If not, you should challenge the condition. If permission has already been granted with the condition attached, submit an application for the condition to be removed and, if the council refuses, submit an appeal.

Planning Obligations & CIL

Planning obligations are also known as developer contributions and Section 106 agreements (named after the relevant section of the Town and Country Planning Act) and they take the form of a legal agreement in which the council secures a contribution towards local infrastructure or affordable housing, for example. The contributions requested must be proportionate to the development proposed and must be necessary to ameliorate the harmful impacts associated with the development. They are rarely required for householder planning applications but are common for developments providing new residential units.

The **Community Infrastructure Levy (CIL)** was introduced by the Labour government in 2010 as a more efficient way of funding local infrastructure. The idea was that councils would set a fixed rate, per square metre, for new development in their area. It meant that there was no longer a need to negotiate and enter into full legal agreements with each individual developer.

Like traditional planning obligations, CIL is mostly paid for by developers (i.e. not homeowners). However, householder extensions are liable for CIL if the development creates additional floorspace of more than 100 square metres. Homeowners don't often realise that some very large extensions (i.e. those with a floor area of 100 square metres or more) are subject to the levy and that they may be charged thousands of pounds when they start work. Designers and planning agents often overlook the possibility that homeowners might be liable for CIL. The actual per-square-metre sum charged varies from council to council.

STEP 4 SUMMARY

1. Some planning applications sail through in eight weeks, but others are tortuous and messy. There are a few steps the humble homeowner can take to ease an application's passage.
2. The validation process can be painful, but it is best to work with validation officers, complying with their requests where possible.
3. The case officer may avoid communication and is likely to ignore the application until a few days before the deadline. Use the site visit as an opportunity to build rapport.
4. Don't worry too much about neighbour objections – they are not usually critical to the outcome.
5. Don't bother with pre-application advice. It is quicker, cheaper and more conclusive to simply submit an application.
6. Contact any internal consultee (the council's tree officer, for example) who might be relevant to your particular proposal. They can be generous with free advice.

Step 5:
Be Prepared to Resubmit or Appeal

Don't be afraid of a planning refusal. If your proposal is ambitious or controversial, a refusal is an almost inevitable part of the journey to getting permission for what you want. A refusal is not final and can be a positive part of the process of inching forward towards approval. So, if you are refused permission, what should you do next?

READ THE OFFICER'S REPORT

The first thing to do is to read the **officer's report**. The decision notice sets out, in summary, the council's reasons for refusing the application. The officer's report provides a much more detailed assessment. Bizarrely, it is not sent to the applicant or their agent when the decision is made and they are not even informed that the report exists. Most councils upload a copy of the report to their website with the final decision notice, but some just place a copy in their file where it is never read by anyone apart from the line manager who authorised the decision (who may not have read it very thoroughly either). It is public information, so look for a copy on the council's website and, if it isn't there, contact the council or your case officer directly.

The officer's report outlines the key planning policies relevant to the application and explains why the application was refused. It set outs all the matters that were taken into account (the material planning considerations discussed in Step 3). The report is wordy, but much of it is pro forma – only relatively small sections are written by the case officer for each application. Scroll through to identify the two or three paragraphs in which the application proposal is assessed.

The officer's report should substantiate fully the council's position. If, for example, your application is refused because the case officer felt that your extension would harm a neighbour's living conditions through a loss of light, the officer's report should explain which neighbour is affected, what part of their property would suffer a loss of light, and how that harm would come about. It should consider whether any harm caused is unacceptable (i.e. whether the harm is sufficient to justify refusal). It should weigh the harm up against any benefits of the proposal (the planning balance).

If the case officer has not assessed the application properly you will find your first clues here. Are the allegations of harm vague and generic? Do they clearly identify what aspects of your development are problematic and how, specifically, neighbours or the streetscene will be affected? You might also find errors in the assessment. For example, the case officer might allege harm to a ground floor dining room window next door, but you know that window serves a (non-habitable) utility room or downstairs WC. It is rare, but not unknown, for case officers to completely misunderstand the nature of a development, to assess the wrong house or to make basic errors about the site and its neighbours.

When clients contact us for advice, many have misunderstood the reasons for refusal. Some obsess about the varied and exaggerated objections made by neighbours, but a brief look at the officer's report reveals that, as is often the way, the case officer attached very little weight to what the neighbours had to say. The officer's report often explains that most aspects of the proposal were found acceptable. Sometimes it is just one, more or less easily resolved, issue that tripped it up.

Some applicants, when refused permission, don't contact us (or any planning consultants) at all. Many accept the wisdom of the case officer or decide that resistance is futile. Some give in. Remember that a refusal is just the beginning. At the very least, before deciding what action to take, if any, it is important to have a good understanding of precisely why your application was refused. Officers' reports are among the most valuable resources in the planning system and it is impossible to fully understand a planning refusal without them.

Ask for a Meeting

If you have read the officer's report and you are not clear about why your application was refused, you are entitled to seek clarification from the case officer. It is a good idea to ask for a quick meeting in the town hall. A meeting is best, but if they are reluctant to commit to one, schedule a phone call. Make extensive notes – it is easy to forget precisely what is said. It is also best to follow up the meeting with an email to the planner summarising the conversation – this creates a permanent (if unofficial) record that you may later use to exert gentle pressure on the case officer, and it also gives the officer an opportunity to clarify or correct their advice, if necessary.

If you have had any dealings with the planners, you will be aware that they can be reluctant to engage. In my experience, however, though they may avoid contact before and during the application process, most are willing to explain a refusal and to provide some direction after a decision has been made. In some cases, relatively small amendments to a scheme will find favour and case officers will not necessarily make this clear unless you press them. When I was a case officer at various local councils, there were many occasions when I refused an application because of an issue that could have been resolved easily, and I would be surprised that the homeowner or their agent did not then get in touch to discuss the problem. I would assume that the homeowner saw the notification that the application had been refused and simply gave up without looking into the reasons.

Case officers are bureaucrats who tend to hide behind their desks. If they have not met the homeowner and no rapport has been developed, it is much easier for them to deliver "computer says no" outcomes. The advantage of a meeting with the case officer is that it humanises you as the applicant, creates some kind of relationship with them, and presents them with an opportunity to use their discretion to grant permission for something they might otherwise have been inclined to refuse.

The simplest way to get planning permission is obviously to give the planners what they want. Endless resubmissions and appeals are a waste of time and energy, and should be avoided.

If the case officer clearly explains why the application was refused and advises informally how it might be revised and improved to find favour, you must decide whether to make those revisions and resubmit, or stick to your guns and appeal the original decision (or both!).

Approach a Planning Consultant

I said in Step 2 that you don't really need a planning consultant for a relatively straightforward householder application, especially if you have chosen a good, local designer who is familiar with the council and its policies. However, the skills of a planning consultant are valuable when things go wrong. They understand how planning departments work, how case officers tick, and how decisions are made in practice. Many have worked in council planning departments as case officers themselves. Above all, they can tell you if (and how) a planning refusal can be reversed. Since the right approval can make such a difference to your family's living conditions and the value of your home, a poorly conceived attempt to overcome a planning refusal without proper professional representation can be costly.

Large consultancy companies charge high fees and are best for larger schemes. Smaller consultancies, including self-employed planners, are probably best suited for householder proposals. Choose a chartered town planner – they have been through a rigorous process of assessment to be elected members of the Royal Town Planning Institute (RTPI). Their membership confirms that they are fully qualified, experienced, knowledgeable, up to date (and insured) planning experts. Chartered town planners must adhere to a code of conduct that specifies standards of professional ethics.

A good planning consultant will:

- review local planning policies and assess their strength, clarity and relevance;
- look up the planning history of your property and other properties in the surrounding area;
- check planning appeals for the council area to see how other proposals have fared; and,
- provide clear and specific advice on your proposal, its chances of success and how it might be changed/improved if necessary.

If the consultant's advice is that you have little chance of obtaining planning permission, there is no point in proceeding but you may have been saved a great deal of money and time. If there is some chance of success, the consultant should be able to explain exactly what your chances are and how they can be maximised. You can incorporate this advice into a planning application or appeal submission, pre-empting and hopefully dodging possible objections.

Most planning consultants will offer basic advice on an application for free, as a way of generating business. However, it can be worth paying a small fee for a more detailed response. Advice given for free can be brief and rushed. There is also an incentive for the consultant to provide advice that generates a fee (i.e. the consultant generates no income if advising you that a proposal is hopeless and should be abandoned altogether). If you are paying a fee for a one- or two-hour review of your case, the consultant may invest more time and energy and produce a more detailed and considered response.

RESUBMIT YOUR APPLICATION

Appealing should be a last resort. It is generally a good idea to keep working with the planners until you reach a stalemate. If they cannot accept an aspect of your proposal that you cannot countenance giving up, the time has come for the decision to be taken out of the hands of the case officer and the council and given to a higher authority. Until that point, it is best to keep working with the planners to find a compromise. Resubmissions are best where the reasons for refusal can be overcome in a way that is acceptable to you. Perhaps the planner has indicated that they will accept an extension just 0.5 metres shorter than what you hoped for or they dislike the flat roof but would approve a more traditional pitched roof. In those cases, though you disagree with the planner's preferences, you might cut your losses, reapply and move on with your life.

It can also be worth resubmitting if you know the council will refuse again, but you want to improve the proposal by responding to at least some of the council's concerns so that you are better placed to win a subsequent appeal.

Even if you do not want to accept the changes that the case officer has recommended (which usually involve making your development smaller), it is a good idea to revise the plans and resubmit them so that you can bank a consent for a smaller scheme and keep it as your fallback position (see Step 3). At the same time, you can appeal the original refusal. If the appeal fails, your backup plan is ready to go as a workable alternative.

If you resubmit your application within 12 months of the previous application being approved, refused or withdrawn, you should not have to pay a second planning application fee to the council (this is known as your "free go"). You can only take advantage of a free go once.

CASE STUDY: CORRECTING THE
WRONG DESIGN PROBLEM

Recently, I was approached by a homeowner in Birmingham who had applied for planning permission for a two-storey side extension on two occasions and been refused both times. His house was on a corner plot, so the extension would be quite visible from the street. The council had refused his first application on the basis that the side extension was too wide and too prominent when viewed from the street. On receiving the refusal, the homeowner's architect had resubmitted the application, changing the flat roof that was initially proposed to a more sympathetic pitched roof design (i.e. a sloping roof).

This did improve the design of the extension but did nothing whatsoever to address the specific concerns raised by the council (which were the prominence and width of the extension). Unsurprisingly, the second application was refused for the very same reasons as the first. When the client approached me, I explained what the council's concerns were and recommended an appeal. Happily, the appeal was successful and the extension was built. It is important to work out exactly what the council's objections are in order to establish whether it is worth resubmitting an application or submitting an appeal – there is little point in amending parts of a proposal to which the planners had no objection.

Clients often ask me whether it is acceptable to resubmit a new application at the same time as appealing a refusal. This is entirely legitimate and a very common strategy. Appeal inspectors will not be more inclined to dismiss an appeal on the basis that the person appealing has a backup plan. Similarly, council case officers should not treat you any differently because you have submitted an appeal against an earlier decision.

Applicants have a right to appeal and it is important to exercise that right where there is a reasonable case to be made. It is also a necessary check on the council's decision-making powers and ultimately leads to better decisions in the long run. In fact, when refusing applications, case officers sometimes remind applicants of their right to appeal, hinting that they are not persuaded of the fairness of their own decision (I used to do this all the time – one of the reasons I left council planning to become a private consultant is that I felt applicants were getting a raw deal, even from me).

In general, when I was a case officer, I welcomed appeals – it was always interesting to see what an independent **appeal inspector** made of a decision I had made. It helped me learn. Having said that, case officers are not rigorously dispassionate – some have a really disappointing tendency to position themselves against applicants and to take the behaviour of some applicants (or, indeed, objecting neighbours) personally. That is a matter for the individual case officer and I would not hesitate to exercise my right of appeal (with or without a revised application running in parallel) if I thought that was the best strategy for me.

In some cases, an appeal is the only way forward. If the planners have taken against several aspects of your proposal or they object to it in principle (for example, their position is that they simply will not allow houses in a certain area to be converted into flats or they will not, under any circumstances, allow single-storey rear extensions to a depth of more than four metres), then revising and resubmitting the application won't work. If you think you have a reasonable chance at appeal, you should pursue it.

Appeal the Decision

If you have been refused permission, you are not persuaded that the decision was fair, and you cannot see a way through by submitting revised plans, you must consider an **appeal**. Appeals are an essential part of the planning toolkit. Whatever we think of the diligence and competence of individual case officers, they are human, they make mistakes, and some of their decisions are not sound. This is particularly the case if you have followed my advice so far. If you have a competent designer, and some effort has been invested in coming up with a sensible proposal, and you have either complied with the council's policies and guidance or can justify any departure from them, you should challenge any refusal.

a) sensible proposal.

b) complian it

Planning appeals in England and Wales are decided by government inspectors working for the **Planning Inspectorate** (also known as PINS), an agency based in Bristol. If you appeal a refusal, the decision is taken out of the hands of your local council and made again by an independent inspector. It is important to note that appeal inspectors are entirely independent and are not connected in any way with your local council.

Increasingly, controversial proposals are approved only at appeal – councils can keep their hands clean by refusing proposals that have generated public opposition, knowing that they will probably be approved through an appeal, if the applicant submits one. This abrogation of responsibility – a kind of "planning by appeal" – is a growing problem and clearly harms the interests of people who do not understand that their refusal can be challenged or do not have the resources to pursue an appeal. In fact, only around 20 percent of planning refusals end up at appeal. Since at least one third of the remaining 80 percent would likely be granted permission at appeal, thousands of homeowners miss out on the planning permission they want because they did not pursue an appeal.

WHAT IS THE SUCCESS RATE?

Around 40 percent of appeals are successful[3]. This is a high proportion, given that all of those proposals were first assessed by a qualified and professional case officer (one assumes) and found to be unacceptable. It is not a good sign that the gatekeepers of our planning system get it wrong almost half the time. To some, 40 percent seems like a small proportion. However, I tell clients not to focus on the headline figure. It is depressed by hopeless appeals submitted by delusional applicants without professional advice or support. Some schemes deserve to fail.

In my experience, if your appeal is well-conceived, you are likely to win. Like the submission of a planning application, there is little point in speculative appeals. The secret to a successful appeal is being right – reasonable

---

3   Source: Planning Inspectorate.

proposals that comply with planning policies will (usually) be approved. My company, Just Planning, submits hundreds of householder planning appeals each year. We only take on appeals that we think will be successful and we win most of the appeals we undertake.

How to Appeal

One can appeal against any refusal of planning permission, a refusal to issue a Certificate of Lawfulness for permitted development proposals (see Step 2), and against **enforcement notices** (see Step 6). One can also appeal against a failure of the council to validate an application, if the council has not made a decision in the usual target timeframes (eight weeks for most smaller applications), and to challenge planning conditions attached to a grant of planning permission (see Step 4).

Appeals for householder planning applications must normally be submitted within 12 weeks of the council's decision (a longer period of six months is allowed for some applications, including all alterations to flats – ask your planning consultant if you are not sure). Appeals against enforcement notices must be submitted before the notice takes effect (around 28 days from when it was served).

Most appeals are determined through the **written representations** procedure, via written arguments put forward by both sides (as well as neighbours and other third parties, where appropriate). The inspector reviews all the written evidence, assesses the application originally submitted to the council and (usually) carries out a brief site visit. The site visit is purely for the inspector to see the site and is not an opportunity for either side to make its case. If you have a planning consultant, they will handle all correspondence and there is little for you, as the client, to do. You may need to provide access to the inspector for the brief site visit but can otherwise just await the decision.

Some appeals involve a formal hearing or public inquiry. These are usually for larger or more complicated appeals where it is difficult for the issues to be explored fully in writing and oral evidence should be heard. It is very rare to have a hearing or public inquiry for a householder scheme. Smaller householder appeals take around three months to be decided (though timeframes vary). Non-householder appeals take around six months. Enforcement appeals take around nine months. PINS (the planning inspectorate) posts current average times on its website (acp.planninginspectorate.gov.uk). Appeals are made online and there is no charge for submitting an appeal (apart from enforcement appeals, under some circumstances).

THE APPEAL STATEMENT

If you are determined to submit your own appeal, PINS will expect you to present **grounds of appeal**. This usually takes the form of a written **appeal statement** summarising your position. An appeal statement usually has the following sections:

- Background information – the name and address of the person appealing (the appellant), the site address, a description of the proposed development, the council's planning application reference number, the date of the decision, and the council's reasons for refusal;
- A description of the site and the surrounding area;
- An outline of the proposed development (what you applied for);
- Relevant planning history (what applications have been decided in the past);
- Relevant planning policies and guidance;
- The case for the proposal (why you think approval should be granted).

SITE DESCRIPTION

In describing the site, provide information that makes it easy for the inspector to identify the right house, but also provide some context. Remember that, for the most part, the inspector will be interested in whether the development harms the character of the area and/or neighbours' living conditions. It is usual to describe the architectural design of the property and the surrounding pattern of development.

- Are the houses similar in size and style?
- Are they evenly spaced out?
- Do they observe a consistent building line or are they scattered and set at angles to each other?
- Have many of the houses been extended or altered?
- Is it a street characterised by variety or uniformity?

It is important to describe the relationship with close neighbours – how far away they are, whether they have been extended, what windows are close to the boundary with your site. You might want to highlight other physical characteristics that might have a bearing on your proposal: the nature of boundary treatments (do very tall hedges or fences separate the plots?), differences in land levels, the relative orientation of the buildings in relation to the passage of the sun during the day.

Finally, the site description should state whether your property is affected by any relevant planning **constraints**. Let the inspector know if your house is locally or nationally listed or if the site is in a conservation area, the green belt or a flood zone, for example. The planning constraints will be listed on the officer's report, so you should not need to carry out your own research (though watch out for careless errors on the case officer's part).

Outline of the Proposed Development

The next section outlines your planning proposal. Try to keep this simple and clear – you want to give the impression that your development is conventional and uncontroversial, not that it is complicated or overly ambitious. So, don't describe it in painful detail. Look at the description in the officer's report for clues. It is usual to provide dimensions (the depth, width and height of your extension) and let the inspector know what materials you propose.

You might also take the opportunity to briefly explain why you need the extra space or how it will improve your living conditions. This is not strictly a material planning consideration (the main issues in householder applications are design and impact on neighbours) and the inspector will not grant you permission on the basis that you *want* or *need* more room. But, if your extension enlarges a poky galley kitchen, for example, or allows your children to each have their own bedroom, it does no harm to point this out, if only as context.

Planning History

The planning history section is where you can let the inspector know about any previous applications that may be relevant to your proposal. If, for example, you initially applied for a larger scheme and it was refused, you may wish to briefly explain the process through which you took the council's concerns on board and have reduced the scale of your proposal. Don't worry about detailing applications that are not really relevant to your current proposals.

If you were recently granted planning permission for something similar (perhaps part of, or a version of, the proposal to which the appeal relates), you should provide details. If you have been granted permission for a development that you have not yet implemented, it is known as an **extant planning permission**. It can be an important material consideration because it may mean that you already have permission for something similar to, or part of, what you are now proposing. It may represent a fallback position

– a development you could build out if the appeal is not successful. If the inspector considers an extant approval to be a fallback position, they will take it into account when making their assessment – if your appeal proposal does not cause significantly more harm than the fallback, it should be approved.

If a previous application is important to the argument you will be making in the appeal, you should provide the inspector with copies of the **decision notice** and the plans for that application. These can be affixed as appendices to your appeal statement. As a general principle, appeal inspectors will not do their own research on a proposal, because the decision should only take into account information provided by either the council or you, the **appellant**, and on which both sides have had an opportunity to comment. The inspector will not therefore download plans for other applications from the council's website and will not look at images on Google Maps or Google Streetview, for example. You must present any information that is important to your case as part of your appeal submission.

PLANNING POLICIES

It is not necessary to copy out all of the council's policies into the planning policy section. The officer's report will summarise the policies on which the application was assessed and the council will send copies of these to the inspector. It is important that you read the policies, however, so that you understand the council's case properly. The planning policy section is also an opportunity to interpret the policies and guidance. For example, if the council has argued that your extended house does not meet a certain criterion, you might point out that the wording of the policy suggests that it is intended to apply to new homes only, not to existing properties that are being extended. Or you might point out that a section of a supplementary planning document includes the wording "in most cases" or "where practical", implying that the guidance should be applied flexibly. There is no need to include a policy section at all if the officer's report has clearly and fairly set out the policies that are relevant to your proposal.

THE CASE FOR THE PROPOSAL

The most important part of your appeal statement, of course, is the assessment section. The process that the inspector will take, and which you should also take in presenting your argument, is to narrow down the issues to the ones (one or two) that are key to the appeal. Say, for example, that the council's only concern is that your rear extension will overshadow a side window in the neighbour's house. This is really the only point that your appeal statement needs to address. You may set out briefly that the council is satisfied that there is no harm the streetscene or to any other neighbouring amenities, but there is nothing to be gained by arguing these points at length – they are not in dispute. I should say that the inspector has the power to assess any and all aspects of the proposal and inspectors have been known to decide that the council's reasons for refusal are unjustified but that there is another, unexpected, reason why planning permission should not be granted. These decisions are rare, though. Most inspectors focus almost exclusively on the council's reasons for refusal.

Sometimes, when I send draft appeal statements to clients for approval, they write back to say that I have not pointed out that the "green roof" and the solar panels they propose will have substantial environment benefits. It is true that environmental sustainability is a pillar of the planning system and the council's planning policies will, somewhere, encourage reductions in carbon emissions, but it is almost never relevant to the issues being considered in a householder planning appeal. If your extension unacceptably overshadows your neighbour, it will be refused permission. If it does not, it may be approved. Associated sustainability benefits do not outweigh harm to a neighbour (and, in any case, could be achieved by extending in a way that does not cause harm to the neighbour, such as reducing the size of your proposed extension).

Your appeal statement does not need to be long. Resist the temptation to ramble, repeat yourself, rant, or otherwise pad it out. It gives the impression that you are not confident in your arguments. Do not criticise the council or the case officer. It just isn't relevant to whether or not your proposal is acceptable in planning terms. To continue the example above, if the main issue is whether your extension will overshadow a neighbour's window, it is clearly irrelevant how long the council took to reach their decision, or that you suspect they have been bribed by the neighbour, or a councillor has exerted pressure, the case officer has made mistakes or told you on the site visit that "it will be approved'" and so on. The inspector's only concern will be to come to an independent, objective view on whether the extension unacceptably harms your neighbour.

Don't get angry. The planning process can be very stressful and many of my clients are enraged by the way they have been treated by the council and their case officer, especially if the case officer has not communicated with them and the decision was unexpected and seems unfair. Remember, though, that the inspector is impartial and will not take sides. They will not share your anger. To reiterate, how the council has behaved is not a material planning consideration. If you feel you have a genuine complaint, consider an application for costs (more on this a little later) or follow the council's internal complaints procedure.

Some appeal statements include information on other proposals for which the council has granted permission or other appeals that have been allowed. These precedents are useful only where they attack directly the specific issues in your appeal. If you are proposing a four-metre-deep rear extension and the council's position is that it will overshadow a window in a neighbour's house, there is no point listing all of the applications for four-metre-deep rear extensions that the council has approved. In refusing your application, the council is not saying that it cannot accept four-metre-deep extensions in principle and will never grant permission for them, it is saying that, in your specific circumstances, the siting of your extension relative to your neighbour's window will give rise to harm.

You should only quote another case for which the council has granted approval where this relationship (between an extension and a neighbour's window) is very similar. A close match will usually be very difficult to find – there are often site-specific circumstances that justify granting permission in one case but not in another (the orientation of the houses relative to the sun, difference in land levels, the height of the extension, the size of the neighbour's window, etc.). Look at the officer's report for both applications to see how they were assessed. Draw the inspector's attention to the other application only if you think the council has been inconsistent in its assessment. Do not worry if your appeal statement does not quote other council or appeal decisions – inspectors often dismiss them as not helpful or relevant; they like to make their own assessments and their own decisions.

SUBMITTING AND MANAGING YOUR APPEAL

A detailed explanation of how to submit and manage your appeal is outside of the scope of this book. You can submit online at acp.planninginspectorate.gov.uk and the website has helpful guidance on how to complete the form. Once you have submitted a householder appeal, you cannot add anything further to your appeal statement, so ensure you submit everything you need to upfront. The council will notify neighbours that an appeal has been submitted and will forward any representations that were received when the application was being considered, but neighbours will not be given an opportunity to comment further at the appeal stage.

Householder appeals relate only to extensions to houses; alterations to flats and all development projects (such as the conversion of a house into flats or the building of a new house) are considered to be full planning appeals. These take a little longer and there is an opportunity for neighbours to make representations and for you to add to your statement after the appeal has been submitted.

The inspector will base their decision on your grounds of appeal and on the information submitted by the council – mainly the officer's report, the relevant policies, and any comments that were made by third parties (such as neighbours or the highways authority) at application stage. The inspector will also carry out a brief site visit. This is not an opportunity for you to discuss the case with the inspector, who will simply turn up and take a quick look at the house and the surrounding area.

THE APPEAL DECISION

Appeals are managed online and all correspondence is emailed to your agent (or to you, if you are appealing on your own behalf). The decision will also be sent by email and will include a fairly detailed report setting out the inspector's reasoning. If permission is granted, there may be conditions attached (as always, pay attention to these – there is more information on planning conditions in Step 4). The appeal decision is your formal decision notice (the council will not write to you separately) so keep a copy of it as evidence that your new development does have planning permission.

If permission is refused, it is important to read the inspector's report fully to understand why you were not successful. It may be that some parts of the development *were* found acceptable or that the inspector has hinted at how the scheme could be redesigned in order to find favour. You cannot, at this stage, communicate with the inspector to obtain further information or to discuss the case in more detail. You do not have a further right of appeal – the only way to challenge an appeal decision is on legal grounds, through judicial review. For this you will need advice from a solicitor or barrister, not a humble planning consultant. Judicial reviews are outside of my area of expertise, but I understand them to be a difficult and expensive process, and not a practical solution for most householders. Having said that, if you are especially aggrieved by the appeal decision or suspect that an error has been made, you should take legal advice.

If the decision hasn't gone your way, don't despair. Appeals are not always a matter of win and lose, they are often a way of evolving a proposal. Sometimes a council has issues with several aspects of a scheme and it is not feasible to correct all to their satisfaction. Though an inspector at appeal might agree with the council that the scheme as a whole must be refused permission, the appeal decision may indicate that the council was wrong to take against some specific aspects of the proposal. An appeal decision is a very important material planning consideration, so anything that the inspector is happy with may be considered settled, even if the appeal is lost.

This is a key point. Imagine that the council has refused permission for a rear extension on the basis that it would be overbearing on your neighbours and represented poor design because of the positioning of the windows. You appeal, and the inspector dismisses the appeal on the basis that the positioning of the windows is, as the council had said, not acceptable. However, in the accompanying report, the inspector makes clear that the council was wrong to conclude that the extension would be overbearing on your neighbours. The council must accept this judgement. In other words, though your appeal has failed, you have resolved the issue of a possible impact on neighbours. You could then submit a new application to the council, altering the positioning of the windows to the case officer's satisfaction, and expect to be granted permission.

CASE STUDY: TRIPPED UP BY TREE ROOTS

Alistair Farmer dreamed of demolishing the cramped bungalow in Northampton that he had been living in for the past twenty years and replacing it with a large, shiny, new two-storey house with a basement and loft rooms. The design was ambitious and a bit unusual, which spooked the case officer. The council refused the application on the basis that the house was too large and would look out of place on the streetscene, and also that the new basement would harm the roots of a nearby protected oak tree.

I prepared and submitted an appeal on his behalf. The inspector decided that the design of the house was acceptable in this location – it would be bigger than many of its neighbours and the neo-classical design approach was a new departure for the area, but the houses along the row already differed in one way or another. Alistair's mini-mansion would not look out of place in this mixture of architectural styles. However, the inspector still dismissed the appeal (i.e. refused to grant planning permission) because she was not satisfied that the aboricultural (tree) reports submitted with the application showed conclusively that the development would not harm the protected tree.

On my advice, Alistair hired a new arboriculturist (tree consultant) to design additional measures to demonstrate conclusively that the tree would be protected. These were submitted along with a new application to the council. I submitted a supporting statement to explain that the inspector had found the design of the house to be acceptable and that the council should not, therefore, continue to object to the proposal on this basis. The application was approved and Alistair and his family are now happily living in their new house (and the tree has survived the basement dig, so far).

As I have said before, more ambitious or controversial proposals rarely sail through the planning process first time. It is usually necessary to try some combination of applications and appeals, refining your design each time. Planning refusals and appeal dismissals are disheartening but can be a productive part of the planning journey. Appeals are not, therefore, the end of the road, but part of the overall planning process. They are a planning tool to be employed where (i) a good, thoughtful proposal has been put forward and unreasonably refused, (ii) the proposal cannot be amended in ways that would be acceptable to both parties and (iii) the decision must be independently reviewed.

WINNING AN AWARD OF COSTS

The appeal inspector has the power to require one party in an appeal to reimburse the other side for the costs associated with the appeal. Costs awards are relatively rare - the general principle is that the parties to an appeal must cover their own costs. However, either party can apply for a costs award if they believe the other side has behaved unreasonably, as long as they can show that this behaviour has led to wasted expense. The decision on a costs application is made by the same inspector who decides the appeal itself. That you win the appeal does not mean that your costs application will be successful – the inspector may decide that planning permission should be granted but will not necessarily reach the further conclusion that the council acted unreasonably in refusing permission in the first place.

It is gratifying for an appellant when the council is required to cover their appeal costs. Costs are awarded in cases where the council was clearly unreasonable in taking the position it did or did not follow the correct appeal procedure (failed to provide information on time, for example, or failed to turn up for the site visit). If costs are awarded, they cover the direct costs of appealing only. They do not include compensation for lost income as a result of any delays or for the cost of the original planning application, for example. Of course, it is not just councils at risk of having to pay out – you can also be held liable for the council's costs if you are deemed to have behaved unreasonably. This sometimes happens where appeals are submitted that had no reasonable prospect of success, for example if an appeal is submitted for the same development that had already been considered, and refused, through a previous appeal.

One final note: it is not always a good tactic to apply for a costs award, even if you are clear that the council has acted unreasonably. Case officers don't always put a great deal of effort into fighting appeals, which is obviously good for the appellant. Sometimes we submit appeals with several thousand words of persuasive argument and the council doesn't respond at all. If you submit an application for costs, however, the case officer may work much harder to justify the refusal of planning permission rather than risk the council having to pay out. The risk of a costs award incentivises them to put more effort into the appeal. For most appellants, the priority is winning the appeal and getting planning permission – the matter of costs is a secondary concern.

Appeal FAQs

Can I Negotiate with the Inspector?

When you submit an application to the council, there are opportunities to negotiate with the case officer and submit revised plans before a decision is made. However, you cannot negotiate with the appeal inspector and you cannot (usually) revise your plans through the appeal process. The purpose of the appeal is to have an independent third party revisit the council's decision. The appeal must therefore be based on the plans that were considered by the council. If you want to make amendments, you need to resubmit an application to the council and, if it is refused again, then appeal.

If the inspector dismisses your appeal (i.e. refuses planning permission), there is no opportunity for a meeting or a conversation to discuss the decision and the inspector will not usually explain what might be acceptable in the future or how, specifically, your proposal could be altered to find favour. The report that is produced along with the appeal decision may, through its assessment of the appeal proposal, suggest how it could be improved, but it will not provide a clear roadmap. If you have been refused permission and you agree with some of the council's concerns – i.e. there are alterations that you yourself would like to make in order to improve the proposal before the plans are considered by an inspector – you must first resubmit your application and obtain a new decision from the council.

Can I Submit an Appeal Myself?

Yes, but don't. Also, be sceptical of your designer's offer to submit your appeal unless they have planning experience and regularly submit appeals for clients. Consult a qualified (chartered) planning consultant. Planners spend their working lives reading application and appeal decisions, reviewing officers' reports and monitoring local plans. They can quickly assess whether your application was well conceived and whether the council's refusal is fair. They will research other decisions in the council area and other appeal decisions.

They will also be aware of, and can look up, the relevant case law. If an appeal has little chance of success, they will tell you, saving you the hassle, time and expense of a fool's errand.

WILL I HAVE TO STAND UP AND MAKE MY CASE?

No, almost all appeals for smaller-scale developments are decided through an exchange of written reports, known as "written representations". I recommend that you hire a planning consultant with experience of householder planning appeals and let them handle the process for you. You will not have to appear in person, give evidence or otherwise need be involved in any significant (or potentially stressful) way. The inspector may want to visit your property, but this is a quick visit and there is strictly no discussion of the case. The inspector will not usually want to see inside your home, they will just want to take a look at the rear garden (or any other outside spaces not visible from the street). Increasingly, inspectors just ask that you leave the side gate open and give your permission for them to enter the rear garden unaccompanied at a pre-arranged time.

Step 5 Summary

1. A refusal of planning permission is not the end of the road: resubmitting an application or appealing a decision can be a constructive part of the planning journey.
2. It is important to inform yourself properly of why your application was refused – read the officer's report and speak to your case officer.
3. Consider paying a small amount for independent planning advice.
4. If your application can be revised in a way that is acceptable to the council and tolerable to you, a resubmission may be successful. If not, an appeal may be the best way to make progress. Even if the appeal is not successful, it may resolve some issues and indicate how further progress may be made.

Step 6:
Beware of Planning Enforcement

The previous chapters have shown how England and Wales have adopted a complicated, overbearing, and intrusive system of planning control. It would have little effect, however, if there weren't means to ensure that people followed the rules. It is clearly in the public interest that developers and homeowners do not just ignore the system and build what they like; it is also important that when planning permission is obtained, the works are carried out exactly as approved.

Every council has a team of planning officers that does not assess planning applications but rather deals with breaches of planning control. This enforcement team receives complaints from members of the public, investigates alleged breaches, and takes enforcement action where necessary and appropriate. Receiving an enforcement visit is an unwelcome surprise but it is not a personal attack. Early action can avoid the situation escalating to an enforcement notice. Don't be tempted to skip this step – read on.

THIS CHAPTER IS FOR YOU

You may not think this section is relevant to you – you play by the book and would never countenance carrying out any kind of development without all the correct permissions in place. Few people start work without planning permission (though it can sometimes be a valid strategy, as we shall see later). However, the complexity of the planning system makes it very easy to run into trouble. Every year, I help hundreds of people who have followed the rules, obtained consent, instructed a builder and, yet, still receive a knock on the door from a planning enforcement officer (they have an unfriendly habit of turning up unannounced).

Many enforcement investigations don't lead anywhere but it is best to have an understanding of how they work and some advice on how to handle the enforcement officer. Some investigations lead to enforcement action – it is surprisingly difficult to build something in exact accordance with a set of plans, and builders may make small adjustments to make life easier. It is easy to overlook a condition or to have misunderstood your permitted development rights.

Anyone carrying out a development should have a basic understanding of how the planning enforcement system works and how to avoid the most common traps. However, enforcement is a complex area of planning law and much of the detail is outside the scope of this chapter. If facing enforcement difficulties, you are strongly recommended to seek professional advice from a chartered town planner or a solicitor with experience of planning enforcement.

WHAT TRIGGERS AN INVESTIGATION?

The enforcement process starts with an investigation, usually triggered by a complaint from a neighbour; councils do not like to make work for themselves and planners do not go looking for breaches of planning control.

The enforcement team is not a planning police force – officers do not patrol the streets. To the surprise of many householders, the planners do not come to check your development after you have finished – there is no formal confirmation that what you have built is in accordance with your planning permission and approved plans.

Building projects are regularly inspected by the council's **building control** officers. However, it is worth reminding ourselves that planning and building control are separate departments of the council, which serve different functions. Building control ensures that building works are carried out to a good standard and that new structures are safe and well-insulated. They are not planners and have no interest in whether or not you have the correct planning consents. Though they come out to inspect your building project, they will not (normally) let you or their planning colleagues know if you are in breach of planning.

Since the council relies mostly on neighbour complaints, the vast majority of breaches never come to the planners' attention and are never challenged. Lots of people carry out works without planning permission, or not entirely in accordance with a planning permission. This is why you can be refused planning permission for developments that other people on your street have carried out, and why it can be dangerous to rely on neighbours' monstrosities as indications of what you might be able to build (this is the "precedent trap" discussed in Step 3). If you see a development and think to yourself, "how on earth did they get permission for that?", the truth is that they probably didn't.

As an aside, the fact that most enforcement investigations are triggered by a neighbour's complaint is a good reason to do what you can to keep your neighbours onside. Planning disputes can get nasty – neighbours don't like the idea of noisy and disruptive building work and the planning application process encourages them to focus on possible harm to them in terms of a loss of light, outlook, and privacy. Take your plans round to your neighbours before you apply and take reasonable measures to keep disruption from building work to a minimum.

HOW DOES AN INVESTIGATION WORK?

Enforcement officers generally just turn up at the property. If permission has been granted for a development, they will bring along a set of the plans and the decision notice. They can see what building works are being carried out and whether they appear to comply with any planning permission that has been granted. This practice of turning up unannounced is controversial. For the case officer, it is the quickest and most direct way to resolve the allegation – they can inspect the building works that have taken place. If the owner is not present, they may be given access to the property by the builders, who are reluctant to resist an officer of the council. Clients often complain to me that it seems unfair they were not present for the first, and fairly crucial, step in the enforcement investigation. It is an ideal situation for the planner, though – they can establish the facts of the case without a lengthy conversation with a panicked and defensive owner.

PLANNING CONTRAVENTION NOTICES (PCNs)

If the site visit does not resolve the question, the council can serve a formal **planning contravention notice (PCN)**. This is a document requiring you to provide information to help the council assess whether a breach of planning control has occurred. You are legally required to reply to the PCN, giving honest and complete answers, within the time limit set out on the notice (usually 21 days). You may be fined a maximum of £1,000 if you do not respond in full and honestly. In practice, though, fines are rare.

PCNs are not usually issued for allegations relating to physical building works. If it is suggested that a recently constructed extension is taller than it should be, for example, the enforcement officer can just measure it. It is a simple matter to establish whether or not there has been a breach of planning control. PCNs are more useful for matters that are not immediately obvious. If it looks like a house is being used as a **house in multiple occupation (HMO)**, i.e. let to several households, the PCN will seek to establish how many people are living in the property, what their relationship is to each other, and when they moved in. In recent years, councils have been tackling landlords renting their properties to holidaymakers on short-let sites like Airbnb. To establish whether or not there has been a material change of use, a PCN can require the owner to provide a list of recent occupants with details of how long each let was for.

If you receive a PCN, it is best to seek professional advice from a planning consultant. The answers you give in your response to the PCN may determine whether further enforcement action is taken and, though your answers must, by law, be complete and truthful, care should still be taken to ensure that you do not unnecessarily incriminate yourself. Sometimes, when I take on an enforcement case for a client, I discover that the responses they gave to an earlier PCN have inadvertently made things more difficult for themselves.

THE OFFICER'S DISCRETION

If, through the site visit and the service of a PCN, the enforcement case officer is satisfied there has been a breach of planning control, they must decide what further action to take, if any. The council's planning enforcement powers are discretionary. There is no obligation to pursue breaches in planning control. They must decide whether taking enforcement action is **expedient**, that is, whether it is in the public interest. There is no point in enforcing against minor breaches where no real harm is caused.

Since case officers have discretion when it comes to enforcement action, there is some hope of influencing their decision. Clearly, whether a breach is minor is a subjective matter. Like most of us, enforcement officers want an easy life. Preparing and serving an enforcement notice is a lot of work. They will not be inclined to take action unless it is necessary and are much more likely to pursue enforcement action if they are under pressure from a third party. If the initial complaint has come from a neighbour and that neighbour is regularly calling up and asking for action, it becomes more difficult for the officer to quietly close the case. A pragmatic officer will consider whether closing the case will enrage the neighbour enough to cause more difficulties than if enforcement action were pursued. Similarly, if local councillors are animated by the breach, it is much more likely that action will be taken. Your own behaviour also matters – officers are naturally more inclined to help people with whom they sympathise or have built up some kind of rapport.

Managing Your Case Officer

Be honest, don't be evasive, and don't be aggressive. Enforcement officers are not the enemy, they are simply doing their jobs. An investigation is not an attack on you personally, nor is it an attack on your character. Remember that you have not committed an offence by failing to obtain planning permission. Enforcement officers are not there to judge, punish or otherwise make your life difficult. Like other public servants, there are there to help. Their greatest frustration is that many of the people they contact immediately become hostile or defensive or, worse, refuse to communicate at all. If you respond to their questions and seek their advice, you are much more likely to have a positive outcome. Most people have good experiences with planning enforcement officers.

If the council makes contact with you, either through an informal letter, a sudden appearance at the property or a formal PCN, it is important to engage early and fully. Try and meet the officer face-to-face and ask them for advice. It is in the interests of both parties that any issues are resolved quickly and smoothly without any further action. Remember that the officer has the power to decide (subject to managers' approval) that it is not expedient (not in the public interest) to pursue any further action. If they decide that a breach has occurred and that it is expedient to take further action, they may be flexible about how the breach is resolved, how much time is given to resolve it, and whether a formal enforcement notice will be served.

CASE STUDY: A TALE OF TWO BRICKS

In 2018, Jonathan obtained planning permission for a single-storey rear extension to his modest Victorian terraced house near Manchester. His neighbour was not pleased that planning permission was granted and was very concerned about this new structure being built on his boundary. One of the things the neighbour did not like was a section of guttering proposed for the side of the extension. Following protracted and difficult conversations with the neighbour, Jonathan agreed to very slightly increase the height of a parapet wall to conceal the offending guttering. This was at the neighbour's request and seemed to placate him.

Some time later, Jonathan was surprised to receive a visit from a planning enforcement officer. The officer explained that a complaint had been received from a neighbour – presumably the very neighbour who had asked for the guttering to be concealed. The officer went into the garden, measured the extension and declared that it was 150mm (the equivalent of two bricks) too tall and that it would have to be altered to comply with the approved plans. Jonathan approached Just Planning for advice and I told him that it was very unlikely the council would take any further action on such a modest and harmless breach, despite what had been said on site. I made contact with the case officer who agreed, after some prodding and gentle persuasion, that enforcement action was not justified and that the case would be closed.

RETROSPECTIVE PLANNING APPLICATIONS

I have explained that the enforcement investigation will seek to establish (i) whether there is a breach of planning and (ii) whether it is expedient (in the public interest) to take any further action. If the breach is very minor and of little consequence – you obtained planning permission for an extension but installed an extra rooflight without permission, for example – no further action is necessary. If the case officer is of the view that the development is entirely inappropriate and that it is unlikely the council would grant planning permission for it, they will probably ask that the development be reversed (that any unauthorised structure is demolished, for example). The timeframe on this is open to negotiation and will depend partly on how successfully you have developed a rapport with the case officer. You are not legally obliged to comply with the case officer's request unless it is presented in the form of a formal enforcement notice (more on this below) – it is simply an attempt to nudge you into complying without further action being taken.

If the case officer believes that planning permission might be granted, you may be invited to submit a **retrospective planning application**. Contrary to popular belief, this is exactly the same as a regular planning application, except that the development is already in place. You submit the same application form, plans and application fee, and the application is assessed on the same policies, as if the development had not yet taken place. In most cases, it is best to submit a retrospective application if invited to do so. If you do not, you are likely to be served with an enforcement notice asking you to reverse, in its entirety, the unauthorised development. Once a notice is served, your options narrow and the opportunity for a negotiated compromise is generally lost. The only circumstances in which I would (very cautiously) advise clients not to submit an application is if we feel that the council is bluffing, in other words they are broadly satisfied that the development is acceptable and that further enforcement action is not justified, but they are erring on the side of caution by asking for a full application. By calling their bluff, they may simply decide to take no further action and close the file.

RETROSPECTIVE PLANNING APPLICATION WITH AMENDMENTS

If submitting a planning application, make sure to secure the services of a good designer and a planning consultant with experience of enforcement matters. Be very wary of relying on the services of anyone who offers to help but does not have direct experience of planning enforcement.

If there are particular aspects of the development that the case officer objects to, or that your planning consultant says do not comply with policy, your retrospective application can propose changes to the completed development. A good planning consultant can help identify the kind of compromises that may ease the passage of your application.

Imagine, for example, that you have built an extension that is both bigger than what was approved and that you finished it with a flat roof, rather than the hipped (sloping) roof the council wanted. You want to avoid reducing the size of the extension, because that would be hugely expensive, but you decide that you would happily replace the flat roof with a hipped roof, which would go some way towards satisfying the council's concerns. In that case, your retrospective planning application would propose retaining the increased size of the extension but replacing the flat roof with a hipped roof. In this example, your planning consultant might even recommend that you submit two applications simultaneously – one to retain the extension exactly as it is (flat roof and all), the other to replace the flat roof with a hipped roof.

If your planning application is refused, you have a right of appeal to the planning inspectorate, as with any planning application (see Step 5). It comes as a shock to some of my clients that the fact that you have submitted a planning application or appeal does not stop the council serving an enforcement notice – it can do so at any time – so it is a good idea to maintain communication with your case officer and request that they hold off any further action until the application and appeal have been decided.

The Awesome Power of an Enforcement Notice

The council's main coercive power is the serving of an enforcement notice. An enforcement notice is a formal legal document alleging a specific breach of planning control and setting out steps for you to remedy that breach within a prescribed timeframe.

The council will serve an enforcement notice if it concludes that you are not likely to reverse the unauthorised development voluntarily and if it is expedient (in the public interest) that you be legally complied to do so. Councils will not normally rush to serve a notice – they are tricky to draft and often lead to unwanted appeals. The government also makes clear to councils that they should only be served as a last resort. They are often served because householders and developers have been uncooperative and have not communicated effectively with the planners, leading them to conclude that a negotiated compromise was not likely.

The notice must take a particular format and include:

- The allegation;
- The steps you must take to comply;
- The compliance period;
- The date the notice takes effect (at least 28 days from when it was served);
- The reasons why the council considers it necessary to serve the notice;
- The precise boundaries of the land to which the enforcement notice relates (shown on a plan attached to the notice).

It is important not to confuse an enforcement notice with an initial letter from the council regarding a possible breach of planning control. Clients often call us to say that they have been served with a notice, when it is in fact an informal letter notifying them that the council is investigating an alleged breach. If you are in breach of planning, but the development could be adjusted to satisfy the council (by reducing the size of an extension, for example) it is important to persuade the case officer to hold off serving an enforcement notice while you come up with a revised proposal and submit a retrospective planning application.

An enforcement notice generally requires that you reverse the unauthorised development in full. The council does not usually allow any further negotiation and, once a notice has been served, has the legal power to refuse to even consider a new planning application for the development. If you do not comply with a notice within the prescribed period, you have a committed a criminal offence and may be prosecuted and fined.

Complying with a notice does not mean that it is discharged. An enforcement notice imposes a continuing obligation to comply with its requirements. In other words, if an enforcement notice is served against the use of an outbuilding as a bedroom and the notice is complied with by removing the fixtures and fittings so that the outbuilding is used once again for storage only, any future breach of the same kind (i.e. using the outbuilding once again as a bedroom) is a breach of the original notice and therefore immediately a criminal offence.

Do Not Ignore an Enforcement Notice

It is almost always worth appealing an enforcement notice. At the very least, appealing it buys you some time – enforcement appeals take 9–12 months to be decided. Once you appeal, the enforcement action is paused and you can retain the unauthorised development while a decision is made. If you do not appeal within the time period set out in the notice itself (usually 28 days), the notice takes effect, and you are obliged to comply with its requirements.

Every year, dozens of people approach me asking for advice on a notice that has already taken effect. Sometimes it has not only taken effect, but the time allowed for complying with the notice (demolishing an extension, for example) has elapsed, and a criminal offence has therefore been committed. A surprisingly large number of people ignore a notice. Some, I think, are paralysed into inaction. Others hope it will just go away. Planning consultants cannot do much to help if a notice has already taken effect, though we can explain what the notice says and what it requires of you. If you wish to challenge it at that stage, however, you need legal advice.

Withdrawal of an Enforcement Notice

Councils will not generally withdraw an enforcement notice after they have gone to the trouble of serving it, unless they discover that they have made an error in the way it is drafted. They are also very unlikely to withdraw the notice if you have not appealed in time, or if the appeal has failed. However, once the appeal has been submitted there is a small window of opportunity for you to persuade the enforcement officer that the notice should be withdrawn.

The secret is to produce a persuasive case, backed up by convincing evidence, that the development is acceptable in planning terms, is not in breach of planning or is immune from prosecution. Enforcement appeals are expensive, stressful, and time-consuming for all parties. Councils know that many people do not appeal enforcement notices or do not put a convincing case forward in the appeal. If you make a professional submission, the council is much more likely to consider whether it is worth proceeding with the appeal and risk losing, as well as the risking the possibility of paying the appellant's costs. If the council decides, in light of your appeal submissions, that it is likely to lose the appeal, it may withdraw the notice.

THE 4-YEAR RULE AND THE 10-YEAR RULE

If a structure is built without planning permission (or not entirely in accordance with a planning consent), it is immune from enforcement action after a period of four years (the "4-year rule"). The change of use of a building into a dwelling is also immune from enforcement action after four years, whether or not the change of use is in breach of a planning condition. Other changes of use (such as the conversion of an office into a shop, for example) are immune after a period of 10 years (the "10-year rule"). A breach of a planning condition also falls under the 10-year rule. The reasoning behind these provisions is to account for developments that were not lawful at the time they were made, but which have not generated complaints or enforcement action over a period of time, and are therefore probably not causing any harm in planning terms.

The rules are controversial among the general public – why should people be allowed to get away with carrying out development without planning permission? It is important to remember that carrying out development without planning permission is not a criminal act. You are entitled to take that risk, knowing that the council may exercise its enforcement powers and you may be forced to take corrective action. It is only when an enforcement notice has been served, takes effect, and is not complied with that a criminal offence is committed.

CERTIFICATES OF LAWFULNESS

If four or ten years have passed and you wish to formally establish that your development no longer needs planning permission, you can apply to the council for this to be confirmed by way of a **Certificate of Lawfulness**. This, also known as a "lawful development certificate", is a document issued by the council to confirm that a development is lawful, i.e. that it meets tests set out in legislation. It is different from a planning permission, which confirms that a development complies with adopted planning policies and is granted express permission.

Applying for a Certificate of Lawfulness is a similar process to applying for full planning permission (one draws up plans, if needed, fills out a form and pays a fee) but the council's discretion is limited – if an application meets requirements in legislation, a certificate must be issued. Importantly, the council has no power to assess whether or not the development is appropriate – i.e. whether it represents good design, harms neighbours, causes parking problems etc – these matters are only relevant to planning applications. If you apply for a Certificate of Lawfulness to establish, for instance, that you built an extension more than four years ago and it is now lawful, the only thing the council can consider is whether or not you have provided sufficient evidence that the structure was built at least four years ago. It cannot refuse to issue the certificate on the grounds that the extension harms a neighbour's outlook, for example.

If the council serves an enforcement notice against a development that you believe to be lawful, you may appeal the notice on the grounds that the development is immune from prosecution by virtue of the 4- or 10-year rules. You are very strongly recommended to secure the services of a planning consultant or solicitor with experience of these kinds of appeals. You can only appeal once, and you will be poorly served if your development was lawful but you did not produce enough evidence to persuade the appeal inspector of that fact.

When applying for a Certificate of Lawfulness or appealing an enforcement notice, you will need strong and persuasive evidence. The council/appeal inspector will not take your word for it. The onus is on the applicant/appellant to show, on the balance of probability, that the four- or ten-year period has elapsed.

CONTINUOUS (UNINTERRUPTED) USE

It is important to note that the four- or ten-year period must be *continuous*, i.e. without interruption. If you built an extension more than four years ago but replaced the roof (perhaps slightly increasing the height of the structure) only two years ago, it is likely that the clock will have restarted and a continuous period of four years has not elapsed. Similarly, if you converted an outbuilding into a dwelling four years ago, you will need to show that it has been occupied (in continuous use) as such for the whole four-year period, up to the date of your application. A decision-maker would expect to see evidence for the full period. If the new dwelling was let you could, for example, present tenancy agreements, bank statements showing rent receipts, and utility bills showing domestic use over the full four years.

CASE STUDY: THE 50-YEAR
BREACH OF PLANNING CONTROL

In 2017, Margaret, an experienced buy-to-let investor with a small portfolio of flats and houses in and around Leeds, bought a house at auction that had been converted into two flats, without planning permission, in 1969. The two flats had been occupied for decades before falling into disrepair and lying empty for the past 10 years. The building was still clearly laid out as two flats – they had their own front doors, kitchens and bathrooms. Margaret's plan was to refurbish and modernise them, and then rent them out.

When doing the legal paperwork after the auction, her solicitor pointed out that there was no planning history to show that the house ever had planning permission to be used as two flats. Margaret was unconcerned – the flats had been there for over 50 years, after all. The solicitor asked the seller to confirm that the council had never expressed any concern about the conversion and that no planning enforcement investigation had ever taken place. He also recommended to Margaret that she apply to the council for a Certificate of Lawfulness (as explained earlier in this chapter) to confirm that the conversion was lawful under the 4-year rule.

The council refused Margaret's Certificate of Lawfulness application on the basis that the unauthorised use had ceased several years ago and was not therefore continuous up to the date of the application. Although the new flats had been created more than four years ago, the council considered that the use had been abandoned. Now that the council was aware that the flats were unlawful, Margaret faced the prospect of being forced to convert the building back into a single-family house – a costly exercise.

She took legal advice and appealed the council's decision. Sadly, the appeal was dismissed. She then contacted Just Planning for help. I called the case officer for an informal chat about the case. She was sympathetic with Margaret's predicament but reiterated that the use was not lawful. She also informed me the council had a planning policy against houses being subdivided into flats, so it was unlikely a planning application would be successful. I nevertheless got the sense that the officer had no appetite for passing the file onto the enforcement team for further action.

Though the certificate application and the appeal had both been unsuccessful, and the council was aware of the breach, it was possible that no further action would be taken – there had been no complaints against the flats after the breach had come to light through Margaret's application. I explained to Margaret that she could choose to take a risk, refurbish the flats and rent them out until such time as an enforcement investigation was launched and the council formally requested that the flats be returned to a single dwelling house. She did as I suggested and has (so far) heard nothing further from the council. Four years from the date on which her first new tenants moved in, as long as the flats have been continuously occupied for the full period, the two flats will once again have met the 4-year rule and be immune from prosecution.

(Almost) Always Appeal an Enforcement Notice

It is usually a good idea to submit an appeal against an enforcement notice. If you do not, it takes effect and you are bound by its requirements. Enforcement appeals are similar to regular planning appeals, discussed in the previous chapter. However, as notices have serious legal implications, it is strongly advised that you employ the services of a planning consultant or solicitor with direct experience of planning enforcement appeals.

There are several grounds on which an enforcement appeal can be made. These are that:

- Planning permission should be granted for the development;
- There has been no breach of planning control;
- The breach alleged in the enforcement notice has not occurred as a matter of fact;
- It is too late for the council to take action (under the 4- or 10-year rules);
- The notice was not properly served;
- The requirements of the notice are excessive;
- The period for compliance is too short.

Enforcement appeals generally take much longer than conventional planning appeals – they usually take around nine months but can take longer than a year. Most appeals for smaller-scale developments are decided through the written representations procedure, where there is an exchange of written reports (i.e. no arguments made orally or in person). Some appeals are decided after a hearing and others after a public inquiry. If you are appealing on the basis that your development is immune from prosecution under the 4- or 10-year rules (see above), it is likely that there will be a public inquiry so that your evidence (and the evidence of any other witnesses) can be tested under oath. You need very strong and persuasive evidence, in my experience, to win an appeal on the basis of the 4- or 10-year rules and, as I have explained, it has best to have professional representation from someone with experience of these kinds of appeals.

Listed Buildings and Protected Trees

Unauthorised works to a listed building or a tree protected by a Tree Preservation Order (TPO) are immediately a criminal offence (since it may not be possible to reverse harm to an older building or restore a tree that has been damaged or removed) and you are at risk of prosecution. The 4-year rule does not apply to listed buildings.

Deliberately Breaching Planning Control

Being in breach of planning control is not a criminal offence. However, if you do not have planning permission, you are at risk of enforcement action, which might mean that you have to reverse the unauthorised development.

In some cases, it is worth taking that risk. Say, for example, that you are building a new house, with full planning permission, and the builder suggests that one of your new ground floor windows would look better if it were half a metre to one side of the position shown on the approved plans. In your view, and in the view of your planning consultant, it is inconceivable that the council would object to this very modest change in the positioning of the window. It is nevertheless, technically speaking, an alteration that needs planning permission. You could apply to the council for a **non-material amendment** (a type of planning application for minor alterations), but that would take time and require a set of plans to be prepared. You might decide, instead, to go ahead with the works without alerting the planners.

You might also decide to take a risk if the cost of reversing the authorised works is low. Say you want to install a new rooflight in the roof of your extension and you decide that, if the council were to take action, the cost of removing it would not be prohibitive. Similarly, you might decide to use a flat roof as a roof terrace without obtaining full planning permission for that use, reasoning that if the council were to take action against the terrace, you could simply stop using it as such (perhaps taking down any railings you have installed), which would not be costly.

The risk of getting caught depends largely on your neighbours – there is the possibility that they will become aware of any breach of planning control and report you. Your neighbours may be aware that you have been granted planning permission for a two-storey house, for example, but they may not have taken the time to forensically inspect the plans. If you have approval for a three-metre-deep extension and you build it to a depth of 3.5 metres, your neighbours may be entirely unaware of the breach. Some neighbours might notice, but simply wouldn't care or would not consider reporting it to the council.

Clearly, larger developments are more costly to remove. It is not a good idea to build a whole new house without permission – your neighbours are likely to notice when it appears, and the cost of demolishing it later would be ruinous. This kind of thing is not unheard of, though. A Surrey farmer, Robert Fidler, famously built a mock-Tudor castle hidden behind hay bales, revealing the development only after a period of four years had passed and he assumed the development would be immune from prosecution under the 4-year rule. After a decade of legal battles, it was established that he could not take advantage of the 4-year rule because he had gone to such effort to conceal the house and deceive the council. The house has since been demolished. Even more extraordinary is the case of Quinn Glass, which built a huge, multi-million-pound, glass container factory near Chester in 2005 without planning permission. It is the largest glass-making plant in Europe. Planning permission was refused twice before finally being approved in 2009.

CASE STUDY: THE RIGHT HOUSE
IN THE WRONG PLACE

Most breaches of planning control are fairly minor – small changes made to an extension as it is being built or a homeowner using a flat roof as a roof terrace, for example. It is rare that whole houses are built without the correct planning permission in place – who would take such a financial risk?

Every year I help homeowners and small developers who face losing a house in its entirety as a result a breach of planning control. In a recent case in Hillingdon, north-west London, a builder had obtained permission to build a bungalow in his sizeable garden and the new house was almost fully completed when a planning enforcement officer visited to say that the house had been built to the correct dimensions – the right height, width, depth, and design – but that he had built it 75cm closer to the rear boundary than he was supposed to. The neighbour to the rear, discovering that the new house was more visible from her rear patio than she expected, had complained.

I visited the site and decided that the difference was not significant and that the council was not likely to take enforcement action. Sadly, I was wrong. I appealed the council's enforcement notice and was delighted when the appeal was successful and planning permission was granted for the bungalow as built. The client learnt a valuable lesson – take very great care to build out any planning permission exactly as shown in the approved plans. Though small variations rarely cause too much trouble, why take the risk?

THE ENFORCEMENT LOTTERY

There were 987 enforcement notices served in England in the fourth quarter of 2019[4]. One hundred and eleven local planning authorities served no notices at all in that period. A further 199 authorities served fewer than 10.

---

4   Source: Ministry of Housing, Communities & Local Government.

The London Borough of Brent served 62, Barnet served 61, and Ealing and Camden served 40 each. Outside London, the most trigger-happy councils were Bradford (22), North Somerset (15) and Leeds (14). The average number of notices issued across England was three per council.

There is therefore something of a postcode lottery when it comes to enforcement. Some councils, especially in London, are more inclined to take action. This is partly, of course, because their districts are more densely populated and they face greater development pressures but it also reflects the culture within individual authorities.

The London Borough of Newham is very comfortable issuing enforcement notices and usually features near the top of the league tables in the government's statistics. In 2016, for example, it issued 300 notices on a long row of properties on Romford Road, a main road in the borough between Stratford and Ilford town centres. The council's motivations were honourable – it wanted to improve the appearance of the main roads into its town centres and there had been an unattractive accumulation of unapproved developments to the ground floor commercial premises – mostly advertisements, signage, canopies, and extensions.

Avoiding the Unforced Errors That Lead to Unexpected Enforcement Action

Most people have no intention of carrying out development without full planning permission, but thousands of people run into trouble every year. Building operations are messy and it is quite common for works to be carried out in ways that do not fully comply with the drawings that were submitted and approved as part of the original planning applications. Builders make small alterations to expedite construction, cut corners or save money. Sometimes they find that works cannot easily be carried out according to the approved plans – the roof design is impractical or the materials proposed are not available, for example. Sometimes there are errors in the plans – land levels are not quite as shown in the drawings or the neighbour's boundary is much closer to the new development than was indicated. Sometimes homeowners request changes as they go along – a new window here or a relocated doorway there.

As I said way back in Step 1, It is very important to invest in high quality plans upfront. If your designer has not measured the site properly and carefully drawn up a proposal that is practical to build, you will inevitably run into difficulties when implementing any planning permission that is granted. Planning drawings are not "indicative" – they are not meant to give a rough idea of what an extension or new dwelling will look like – they must be strictly accurate. If the council grants permission because the house you intend to build will be the same height as an existing house next door, you clearly risk enforcement action if your designer overestimated the height of the building next door, and your new house – though exactly as tall as you proposed it would be – nevertheless rises significantly above your neighbour's, thereby looking out of place on the streetscene.

Most of the clients who contact us having run into trouble with enforcement have carried out a development believing it to be permitted development (PD), only later to discover that it is not. In Step 2, we looked at the various reasons why PD rights might not be available: they are available to houses but not flats, they are restricted in conservation areas, they may be removed by an earlier planning condition or by an Article 4 Direction. These problems are avoided by applying for a Certificate of Lawfulness before starting works.

Homeowners also run into problems when they build something that is almost, but not quite, PD. The most common errors are roof extensions that exceed the 40- or 50-square-metre volume limit or rear dormer windows that are not set back 20 centimetres from the eaves. It is important to understand the PD criteria fully, to work to detailed plans, and to obtain a Certificate of Lawfulness confirming that your proposal is lawful. Do not assume that the planners will look past minor infractions – the PD limits are absolute and failure to comply in every detail exposes you to the possibility of enforcement action. Although very few of our clients end up having to demolish extensions (or, indeed, whole houses) a small minority do, and it is a stressful and expensive experience.

Step 6 Summary

1. Don't assume that you are not at risk of enforcement action – planning is complicated, and it is easy to fall foul of the rules. It could happen to you!
2. Planners don't go looking for trouble – investigations are usually triggered by a neighbour's objection, so keep your neighbours onside.
3. If an enforcement officer comes knocking, work with them to resolve any issues – they are not the enemy.
4. Apply for planning permission retrospectively, if necessary and appropriate.
5. Never ignore an enforcement notice – get professional advice and (usually) appeal.
6. In some circumstances, one can choose to breach planning control deliberately – but usually where the risk of getting caught is small and the cost of having to reverse the breach is low.

Planning Hacks:
A Summary of My Top Tips

Congratulations on making it this far! The following is a summary of my top tips for getting permission for the extensions of your dreams, taken from the six-step programme set out in the previous chapters.

Step 1: Choose the Right Designer

- Invest time and effort in finding the right designer. This first step is crucial – a poor choice will hobble the project from the start.
- The best designers are local – trudge through your council's online planning database to find which designers regularly submit applications in your area and have a high success rate.
- Expect your designer to make creative suggestions and be willing to push back on some of your own expectations.
- Check the quality of their drawings (do the drawings appear attractive, are they reasonably sophisticated and detailed?) and quiz them on their knowledge of local planning policies.
- Think carefully about what kind of extra space you need. Don't sacrifice the external aesthetics of your property on a quest for enormous extensions. Big isn't always better!

STEP 2: EXPLOIT PERMITTED DEVELOPMENT RIGHTS

- It is much easier to extend under permitted development (PD) rights than apply for full planning permission – as long as you follow the criteria, you already have permission.
- PD rights are also quite generous – you can build larger roof extensions and ground floor rear extensions than council planners would usually allow.
- The most popular PD right is the humble single-storey rear extension. This can be up to four metres deep, or up to eight metres using the new larger home extension scheme.
- The second most popular is the rear dormer. This can take up almost all of the rear roof slope of your house, allowing you to add an extra floor and a couple of extra rooms.
- Be careful – mistakes can be stressful and expensive. If you build an extension that does not quite comply with the PD criteria (it is a little too high, for example) it is not lawful, and the council may ask you to demolish it. Getting it right is especially tricky with dormer extensions.
- Remember that only houses have PD rights, not flats. Some rights do not exist in conservation areas and other areas with special designations. Some rights have been removed by a planning condition or by an Article 4 Direction.
- The government is continuously expanding PD rights as a way to sidestep the planners – look out for announcements on new rights that you might be able to take advantage of.
- Always apply for a Certificate of Lawfulness before starting work. This asks the council to confirm that your proposals comply with the criteria and are definitely PD.

Step 3: Understand How Planning Decisions Are Really Made

- Planning applications are assessed against planning policies. National planning policies are set out in the National Planning Policy Framework (NPPF). In London, there is also a regional policy document, the London Plan. Each council has its own planning policies, set out in their development plan. Councils may also have supplementary planning documents.
- Familiarise yourself with the relevant policies. The policy documents are available online, or call/email the duty planning officer for advice. Also check out the officers' reports for similar applications for information on relevant policies and guidance – officers' reports are a priceless planning resource.
- As well as planning policies, the council takes account of other planning considerations – anything else that is relevant to the decision. The various considerations are weighed up in the planning balance.
- Case officers prefer to adhere closely to the planning policies and avoid making exceptions to these policies on the basis of other material considerations. When councils unfairly refuse permission, it is often because they are unwilling to make an exception to their policies.
- The two main issues in householder planning applications (i.e. applications for extensions) are the design of the development, and its impact on neighbours' living conditions in terms of a loss of light, outlook and privacy.
- What other people have built nearby is important, but not decisive (precedent doesn't work in the way people think it does). The planning history for your own site is also a consideration, especially if it gives you a fallback position.

STEP 4: APPLY TACTICALLY AND EFFECTIVELY

- Validation is a pain in the posterior but validation officers are the gatekeepers of the planning department and we have little choice but to work with them to try and comply with any (unreasonable) demands.
- Case officers don't really like communicating with applicants and their agents and they are under no obligation to let you know whether you are likely to get approval before the decision is actually issued. The best time to build some rapport and try to influence them is on the site visit.
- Neighbour objections are not critical – don't worry too much about them. Case officers will make their own minds up about your proposal. However, no one likes neighbour disputes and, in some instances, neighbours can sway a decision. It is best to forewarn your neighbours of your application – pop round with your plans and a bottle of wine.
- Pre-application advice is pointless, unless your application is especially complicated or controversial. It is cheaper, quicker, and more effective to submit a full application.
- If your proposal raises issues of flood risk or harm to a tree protected by a Tree Preservation Order, for example, make contact with the relevant council officers before you apply. They can be surprisingly helpful (in contrast to their jaded planning colleagues).
- Don't withdraw your application, unless it is part of a strategy to keep your case officer sweet. You will lose your right of appeal and gain very little.

Step 5: Be Prepared to Resubmit or Appeal

- A refusal of planning permission is not the end of the road. For a more ambitious or controversial proposal, refusals are an almost inevitable part of the process of inching forward towards an approval.
- If your application is refused, you must first read the officer's report. It is a document written by your case officer explaining in some detail how your application was assessed and why it was refused.
- Case officers will normally agree to a phone call or face-to-face meeting after a decision. You are entitled to ask for clarification on the reasons for refusal. The case officer may have helpful suggestions.
- Hire a planning consultant. Consider paying for an hour of formal advice, rather than asking for free initial advice (which might be biased in favour of recommending whatever generates a fee). Chartered Town Planners meet minimum standards of competence and professionalism.
- Resubmitting your application only makes sense if the amendments you propose (usually making your extension smaller) are likely to be approved the second time round. In many cases, homeowners resubmit and are simply refused a second time. Tinkering with the proposal will not usually be enough.
- You should appeal the decision if the council will not accept your proposal and you are not willing to alter it in a way that the council would approve of. Around 40 percent of appeals, and a much higher proportion of "well-conceived" appeals, are successful.
- Even if the appeal is not successful, it can be part of the process of developing your proposals. The appeal inspector might dismiss the appeal overall, but express satisfaction with certain aspects of the design, for example.

STEP 6: BEWARE OF PLANNING ENFORCEMENT

- Every year, I help hundreds of homeowners who have unexpectedly and inadvertently run into planning enforcement problems. It is stressful and potentially expensive, therefore it is important to understand enforcement before embarking on a building project.
- It is surprisingly easy to be in breach of planning control without meaning to be. Your builder may have constructed some part of your extension in a way that deviates from the plans that were submitted to the council. Or you may have built something under permitted development which does not fully comply with the relevant criteria.
- The council's enforcement officers do not patrol the streets looking for breaches of planning control. In most cases, enforcement investigations are triggered by neighbour complaints.
- A planning contravention notice (PCN) is a formal request from the council for information about a possible planning breach. You must respond and must give honest answers. Seek professional advice from a planning consultant.
- Enforcement action is discretionary – the council does not need to take action, even if a breach has occurred. Action should only be taken where it is expedient. Work with your enforcement officer to find a solution – they are there to help.
- You may need to submit a retrospective planning application. This could include some amendments to what you have built, if this will help you get the application approved.
- If an enforcement notice is served, you should consider an appeal. Do not ignore the notice – failure to comply within the prescribed timeframes is a criminal offence. Always seek professional advice.
- It is not an offence to be in breach of planning (only to fail to comply with an enforcement notice). Minor breaches can therefore be justified – weigh up the likelihood of the council becoming aware of them and the cost of having to reverse any authorised works.

- Breaches of planning permission are safe from prosecution (i.e. become lawful) after four years (for building works and the creation of new dwellings) or 10 years (for changes of use) – but seek advice before assuming that a development is lawful on this basis.

Glossary

Agent – someone who acts for an applicant or appellant in a planning context. It is usually the architect or designer, or a planning consultant.

Appeal – if planning permission is refused, you can submit an appeal against the decision to the planning inspectorate, a central government agency. You can also appeal against an enforcement notice or against a refusal to validate a planning application.

Appeal inspector – the person appointed to determine an appeal.

Appeal statement – a document that sets out your grounds of appeal and is considered by the appeal inspector when they make their decision.

Appellant – an individual or organisation appealing a planning decision.

Applicant – an individual or organisation applying for planning permission or for a Certificate of Lawfulness.

Arboricultural report – also known as a "tree report", it provides information on the care, maintenance and management of trees on a site and provides an assessment of whether a proposed development would cause harm to trees.

Architect – architects design and create plans and technical drawings of buildings. Only persons who are on the Architect Register can use the term architect, but there are no restrictions on who can prepare planning drawings or submit planning applications.

Area of Outstanding Natural Beauty (AONB) – land protected to conserve and enhance its natural beauty. Tighter planning controls apply in AONBs.

Area of special character – areas identified by a local council as having a special character or appearance.

Article 2(3) Land – national parks and The Broads, Areas of Outstanding Natural Beauty, conservation areas and World Heritage Sites. Some permitted development rights do not apply in article 2(3) areas.

Article 4 Direction – used by local planning authorities to remove specific permitted development rights in particular areas. For example, an Article 4 Direction might remove permitted development rights to change one's windows in a conservation area.

Beds in sheds – refers to the use of outbuildings for living accommodation, usually without planning permission.

Breach of planning control – development carried out without planning permission, not fully in accordance with a planning permission or in breach of conditions attached to a planning permission.

Building control – a local authority function that ensures new development meets certain standards of safety and performance. It is a separate function to planning and the two should not be confused.

Case officer – an officer of the local authority who assesses planning applications (also known as a "planner" or "planning officer").

Certificate of Lawfulness – a type of application in which the applicant seeks confirmation that a development is lawful. It is also known as a "lawful development certificate". A certificate of lawfulness application may be submitted to establish whether a proposal is permitted development, for example, or that a development has been in place for several years and is now immune from planning enforcement.

Character appraisal – a document prepared by the local authority setting out the special characteristics of a conservation area.

Chartered town planner – a planning consultant who is a member of the Royal Town Planning Institute (RTPI).

Community Infrastructure Levy (CIL) – a sum payable on some developments after planning permission is granted and when works start on site. It is levied only on certain types of proposal and rarely payable on householder applications.

Conditions – restrictions attached to a planning permission. Conditions are listed on the decision notice and sometimes require you to carry out specific actions before starting work.

Conservation areas – areas designated by the local authority for their special architectural or historic interest. The council has a duty to preserve or enhance the character or appearance of these areas.

Constraints – planning constraints are restrictions that affect a site, such as its location in conservation area or a flood zone.

Core strategy – one of the names used for part of a council's development plan, i.e. its collection of planning policies. The core strategy usually contains the higher level, more strategic policies.

Crown roof – a roof design comprising conventional roof slopes with an area of flat roof on top. It allows for buildings to be wider and deeper without the roof becoming too tall.

Curtilage – the area around, and intimately associated with, a dwelling. It is usually, but not necessarily, all of the land around the property (its front, side and rear gardens).

Decision notice – The written decision issued by a local planning authority in response to a planning application.

Delegated powers – the powers of the planning team to make a decision on a planning application without deferring to the planning committee of elected councillors.

Designer – the person or company who prepares plans and submits an application, often an architect or draughtsperson.

Development management policies – one of the names used for part of a council's development plan, i.e. its collection of planning policies. Development management policies usually provide specific policies on various types of development.

Development plan – the collection of planning policies adopted by a planning authority and the starting point for planning decision making.

Dormer – an extension to the roof of a building, with a window.

Double dormer – an extension to both the main roof of a house, and to a secondary, lower roof.

Duty planning service – a service provided by local planning authorities whereby case officers provide informal planning advice, either in person in the council offices or over the telephone.

Eaves – that part of the roof that overhangs the wall of the building and to which gutters are often attached.

Elevation – a view of a building from one side. The front elevation of a house is the front of the house, for example.

Enforcement – planning enforcement is a local authority function that deals with breaches of planning control.

Enforcement notice – a formal legal document served by a local planning authority when it believes that there has been a breach of planning control. The notice sets out the allegation, the reasons for serving the notice and what is required of the recipient in order to resolve the breach (which might be to demolish an unauthorised extension, for example).

Expedient – whether it is in the public interest for the local planning authority to take enforcement action against an alleged breach of planning control.

Extant planning permission – a 'live' planning permission, i.e. a permission that was granted, has not expired and has not yet been implemented.

Fallback position – an alternative option that an applicant or appellant could pursue if planning permission is not granted. It is usually another extant planning permission or a development that could be carried out under permitted development rights.

Flood Risk Assessment (FRA) – an assessment that is carried out and submitted with a planning application when development is proposed in a flood zone.

Flood zone – an area identified by the Environment Agency (a central government body) or by the council as being at risk of flooding.

General Permitted Development Order (GPDO) – legislation that grants planning permission in advance for certain types of development, known as permitted development, subject to various limitations and conditions.

Green belt – a specific planning designation for land that should be kept open and undeveloped. New development is prohibited in the green belt, with limited exceptions (including modest extensions to existing dwellings).

Grounds of appeal – the arguments on which a planning appeal is made.

Hip-to-gable – a form of roof extension where the side slope is extended out to create a gable end.

House in multiple occupation (HMO) – a dwelling that is not occupied by a single family or household, but by three or more unrelated individuals in separate households.

Larger home extension – a ground floor rear extension to a house with a depth of up to six metres (eight metres on a detached house). It is a form of permitted development, though subject to an application for prior approval and the neighbour consultation scheme.

Listed building – a building designated and given special planning protections as a result of its special architectural and historic interest.

Local list – a formally adopted document that sets out what the council requires to make an application valid, i.e. what plans, information and supporting documents are required for different types of planning applications.

Local plan – the collection of planning policies prepared by a local planning authority.

Local planning authority – the public authority that exercises planning functions in particular areas. In most cases it is the planning body of a district or local council but can also be a county council (for waste and mineral matters, in some cases). The National Parks and the Broads authority are also local planning authorities.

London Plan – a planning policy document setting out planning policies for London. It should be read alongside the local planning policies prepared by each of the individual London councils.

Material planning considerations – issues that are relevant to the assessment of a planning application, such as planning policies, the property's planning history, the design of the proposal and its impact on neighbours.

National Planning Policy Framework (NPPF) – the National Planning Policy Framework sets out government's planning policies for England and how these are expected to be applied.

Neighbour consultation scheme – The process by which a council consults neighbours upon receipt of a prior approval application for a larger home extension (i.e. an extension to a depth of up to six or eight metres). If neighbours do not object, the extension is considered to be permitted development. If an objection is received, the council must assess whether the extension would harm neighbours' living conditions and therefore whether prior approval should be granted.

Neighbourhood plan – a planning policy document produced by a community to manage development in their area. It forms part of the development plan.

Non-material amendment – a type of planning application is which minor or uncontroversial amendments are sought to a development that was previously approved. For example, if you obtained permission for a rear extension and later decided you wanted a smaller rear window than was shown on your plans, you might apply for a non-material amendment to adjust the plans.

Office-to-residential conversion – the conversion of office space into new homes, commonly through a 'light touch' prior approval application relating to permitted development rights, rather than a full planning application.

Officer's report – the report written by a case officer when recommending a planning application for approval or refusal. It is a very useful resource, because it gives detailed information on how the application was assessed and how the decision was reached.

Other material considerations – other planning considerations, apart from adopted planning policies, that are taken into account when assessing a planning application.

Outrigger – the term used for a rear projection behind a building (a kind of extension to the building) – usually it is less wide or less tall than the main part of the building. Outriggers are common on Victorian terraced houses.

Permitted Development (PD) rights – rights set out in the General Permitted Development Order allowing development to be carried out without the need to apply for planning permission.

Planning balance – the weighing up of various (often competing) considerations when assessing a planning application.

Planning committee – the committee of elected councillors who decide planning applications. In practice, most small applications are not decided by the committee, but by the planning officers under delegated powers.

Planning contravention notice (PCN) – A notice served by the planning enforcement department which requires the recipient to provide specified information on a property or development. It is a criminal offence not to respond to a PCN, or to provide inaccurate information. Enforcement officers use the response to the PCN to work out if a breach of planning control has taken place and what the nature of the breach is.

Planning enforcement – a council function that investigates and seek to remedy breaches planning control.

Planning Inspectorate (PINS) – a government agency that decides planning appeals in England and Wales.

Planning obligations (also known as developer contributions or "Section 106 Agreements") – private agreements between local authorities and developers that are attached to a planning permission and commit the developer to build infrastructure, for example, or provide affordable housing.

Planning policies – the policies taken into account by decision-makers (planning officers and appeal inspectors) when assessing planning proposals.

Planning portal – a website which provides information on the planning system and on which planning applications can be submitted (www.planningportal.co.uk).

Planning statement (or supporting statement) – a document that is submitted with a planning application to explain and promote the proposed development.

Pre-application advice – a service offered by councils in which advice is given on a proposal before a full planning application is submitted.

Precedent – a previous development or planning approval that might be considered an example or guide to what might be acceptable elsewhere in similar circumstances.

Pre-commencement condition – a form of planning condition requiring that particular details of a development be submitted to and approved by the council before development starts. To seek approval, one must submit an "approval of details" (also known as a "discharge of condition") application.

Prior approval – an approval that must be obtained from the local planning authority in respect of specified aspects of a development before it be can be carried out as permitted development.

Removal or variation of a condition – a type of planning application in which you apply to delete or alter the wording of a condition attached to a previous approval.

Retrospective planning application – an application submitted after the development has started.

Ridge – the highest point (apex) of a roof.

Side return – the undeveloped area next to an outrigger at the rear of a building.

Site visit – the visit to an application site undertaken by a council case officer or other decision maker as part of the assessment process.

Subordination – the extent to which an extension is secondary to, or less prominent than, the building that is being extended. Also known as subservience.

Supplementary planning document (or supplementary planning guidance) – specific guidance for applicants. It is similar to planning policies, but more detailed and more specific to particular types of development. It does not have the same power as planning policies – it is guidance only, though it is a material consideration in planning decisions.

Terracing effect – where two houses with a gap in between them both extend into this gap, giving the impression that the houses are terraced.

Tree Preservation Order (TPO) – protection given to specific trees or groups of trees. Permission is required to carry out works to a tree protected to a TPO. It is a criminal offence to carry out works without permission.

Validation (of a planning application) – the first process after an application is received by a council, in which they assess whether it is complete, has no obvious errors and that the correct fee has been paid.

Written representations – the most common procedure by which planning appeals are decided, by an exchange of written reports. The other procedures are hearings (where representations are made in person) and public inquiries (where evidence is given under oath).

Planning Resources

For planning advice, news and updates:
martingaine.com

Just Planning (Martin Gaine's planning consultancy)
www.just-planning.co.uk

Just Planning on Facebook (for regularly updated planning news and advice)
www.facebook.com/justplanning

Architects' Register
www.architects-register.org.uk

Environment Agency Flood Zones
flood-warning-information.service.gov.uk/long-term-flood-risk

General Permitted Development Order (latest available version)
www.legislation.gov.uk/uksi/2015/596/contents

Government Guide to Planning Appeals
www.gov.uk/appeal-planning-decision

Historic England (for records of listed buildings)
historicengland.org.uk/listing/the-list

Interactive House (guide to permitted development)
interactive.planningportal.co.uk

National Planning Policy Framework
assets.publishing.service.gov.uk/government/uploads/system/uploads/
attachment_data/file/810197/NPPF_Feb_2019_revised.pdf

Planning Inspectorate (for appeals)
acp.planninginspectorate.gov.uk

Planning Portal (for submitting planning applications)
www.planningportal.co.uk

Technical Guidance (guide to permitted development)
www.gov.uk/government/publications/permitted-development-rights-for-
householders-technical-guidance

MARTIN GAINE is a chartered town planner and chief executive of Just Planning, a planning consultancy focused on helping homeowners and small developers navigate the planning maze. He worked for many years as a council case officer before realising that some applicants were getting a raw deal from the planning system. He founded Just Planning to provide them with a source of good quality, independent advice.

Martin read Politics, Philosophy and Economics (PPE) at the University of Oxford and completed a master's degree in planning at the University of Reading, where he was awarded a distinction. He has a keen interest in property, development and planning and writes about planning issues. His work has been recognised in articles by the Mail on Sunday, The Times and The Telegraph. He also contributes to the 'Ask the Expert' section of the Sunday Times Home supplement, responding to planning queries sent in by readers.

For regular planning updates, sign up to Martin's newsletter:
martingaine.com

For bespoke planning advice on specific planning problems:
martingaine.com/askmartin

To keep up to date with planning news:
facebook.com/justplanning
just-planning.co.uk/news

(84)85

$$\underline{2 \ \ PRIME}$$
$$1$$

DESIGN + APPEARANCE.

IMPACT ON NRs.

a) DOESN'T HARM STREET SCENE.

a) overshadow NRs WINDOW.

B) HIGH QLTY DESIGN

C) RESPECT & REFLECT CHARACTER OF LOCAL AREA.

D) REINFORCE LOCAL DISTINCTIVENESS.

E) PROPORTIONATE IN SIZE + SCALE.

F) USE APPROPIATE MTRL.

G) $\tilde{N}$ TO NRING HOUSES.

— HELPS PROTECT CHARACTER + APPEARANCE OF AREA.

H) PROPOSED DEVL FITS IN WITH IMMEDIATE SURRONDINGS

I) IT IS $\tilde{N}$ IN HTGHT DEPTH + WIDTH TO ADJOINING BLDG. FOLLOWS the bldg line + architectural style. ⑧⑥ RESPECT XISTING PATTERN OF DEVLLO mt

6) continues pattern of developmt falls in place.

-- VARIETY OF BLDG STYLES +
   VOCABULARY (87) A   89--A
- Surrounding pattern of developmt
- not oversized or out of place +
  fits in with character of the area
  → developmt of an abandoned
                          site

Printed in Great Britain
by Amazon

66059245R00132